SPECTRUM®

Phonics

Grade K

Spectrum®
An imprint of Carson-Dellosa Publishing LLC
Greensboro, North Carolina

Spectrum®
An imprint of Carson-Dellosa Publishing LLC
P.O. Box 35665
Greensboro, NC 27425 USA

11-364137811

Table of Contents

Index of Skills

Phonics Grade K

Numerals indicate the exercise pages on which these skills appear.

Auditory Skills

Associate sounds with letters—12, 13, 15, 16, 18, 19, 21, 22, 24, 25, 26, 28, 29, 30, 32, 33, 35, 36, 38, 39, 41, 42, 44, 45, 46, 48, 49, 51, 52, 54, 55, 57, 58, 59, 61, 62, 63, 65, 66, 68, 69, 71, 72, 74, 75, 76, 78, 79, 80, 82, 83, 85, 86, 88, 89, 91, 92, 94, 95, 96, 97, 98, 99, 104, 105, 106, 107, 108

Discriminate initial sounds—12, 15, 16, 18, 19, 21, 22, 24, 26, 28, 29, 30, 32, 33, 35, 36, 38, 41, 42, 44, 45, 46, 48, 49, 51, 52, 54, 55, 57, 59, 61, 62, 63, 65, 66, 68, 69, 71, 72, 74, 75, 76, 78, 80, 82, 83, 85, 86, 91, 92, 94, 95, 96, 97, 98, 99, 104, 105

Discriminate final sounds—88, 89, 96, 106, 107

Discriminate medial vowel sounds—13, 25, 26, 39, 58, 59, 79, 80, 108

Following directions—all activities

Recognize rhyming words—13, 25, 39, 58, 79

Visual Skills

Discriminate letters—11, 14, 17, 20, 23, 27, 31, 34, 37, 40, 43, 46, 47, 50, 53, 56, 60, 63, 64, 67, 70, 73, 76, 77, 81, 84, 87, 90, 93, 96, 100, 101, 102, 103, 108, 109

Discriminate pictures—9, 10

Motor Skills

Coordinate eye-hand movements—6, 7, 8, 30, 46, 63, 76, 96

Trace and/or write letters—12, 15, 16, 18, 19, 21, 22, 24, 28, 29, 32, 33, 35, 36, 38, 41, 42, 44, 45, 48, 49, 51, 52, 54, 55, 57, 61, 62, 65, 66, 68, 69, 71, 72, 74, 75, 78, 80, 82, 83, 85, 86, 88, 88, 91, 92, 94, 95, 97, 98, 109, 110

Oral Language and Vocabulary Skills

Identify objects—12, 13, 15, 16, 18, 19, 21, 22, 24, 25, 26, 28, 29, 30, 32, 33, 35, 36, 38, 39, 41, 42, 44, 45, 46, 48, 49, 51, 52, 54, 55, 57, 58, 59, 61, 62, 63, 65, 66, 68, 69, 71, 72, 74, 75, 76, 78, 79, 80, 82, 83, 85, 86, 88, 89, 91, 92, 94, 95, 96, 97, 98, 99, 104, 105, 106, 107, 108

Letters and Sounds

a—11, 12, 13, 26, 99, 101, 108, 109, 110

b—14, 15, 16, 30, 97, 98, 100, 104, 109, 110

c—17, 18, 19, 30, 101, 103, 109, 110

d—20, 21, 22, 30, 98, 101, 109, 110

e—23, 24, 25, 26, 99, 108, 109, 110

f—27, 28, 29, 30, 101, 102, 104, 109, 110

g—31, 32, 33, 46, 98, 100, 106, 109, 110

h—34, 35, 36, 46, 104, 109, 110

i—37, 38, 39, 59, 99, 102, 108, 109, 110

j—40, 41, 42, 46, 97, 100, 102, 109, 110

k—43, 44, 45, 46, 97, 101, 103, 107, 109, 110

l—47, 48, 49, 63, 106, 109, 110

m—50, 51, 52, 63, 100, 102, 109, 110

n—53, 54, 55, 63, 105, 109, 110

o—56, 57, 58, 59, 99, 102, 108, 109, 110

p—60, 61, 62, 63, 98, 102, 107, 109, 110

q—64, 65, 66, 76, 97, 101, 105, 109, 110

r—69, 70, 71, 76, 97, 98, 100, 104, 106, 109, 110

s—70, 71, 72, 76, 97, 98, 101, 102, 107, 109, 110

t—73, 74, 75, 76, 97, 98, 100, 103, 107, 109, 110

u—77, 78, 79, 80, 99, 103, 108, 109, 110

v—81, 82, 83, 96, 97, 103, 106, 109, 110

w—84, 85, 86, 96, 100, 103, 105, 109, 110

x—87, 88, 89, 96, 109, 110

y—90, 91, 92, 96, 98, 103, 109, 110

z—93, 94, 95, 96, 97, 105, 109, 110

Short Vowels

a—12, 13, 26, 99, 108

e—24, 25, 26, 99, 108

i—38, 39, 59, 99, 108

o—57, 58, 59, 99, 108

u—78, 79, 80, 99, 108

Tracing and Coloring

Directions: Trace the dotted lines to finish the picture. Then, color the picture.

Start here.

Tracing and Coloring

Directions: Trace the dotted lines to finish the picture. Then, color the picture.

Start here.

Left to Right

Directions: Trace each dotted line from left to right.

Same

Directions: Circle the two pictures in each row that are the same.

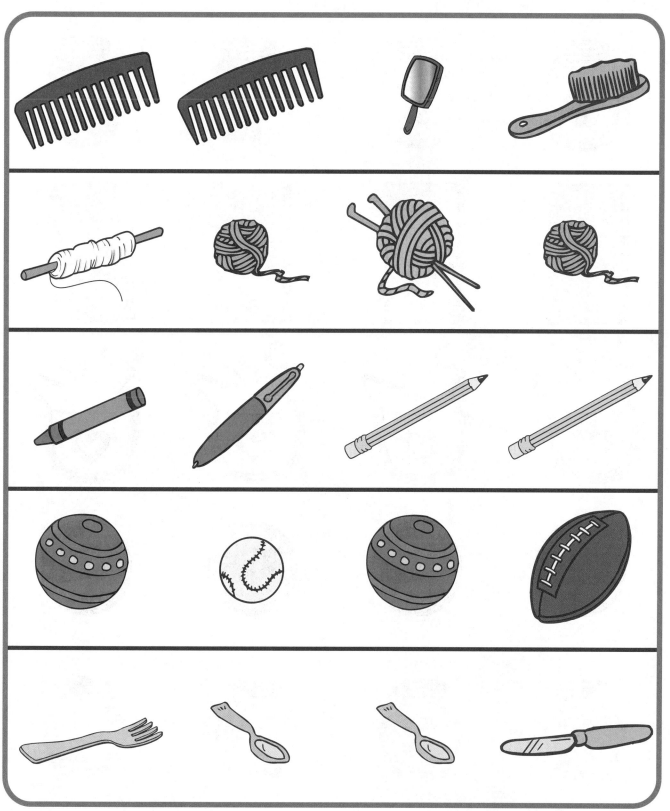

Different

Directions: Draw an **X** through the picture that is different in each row.

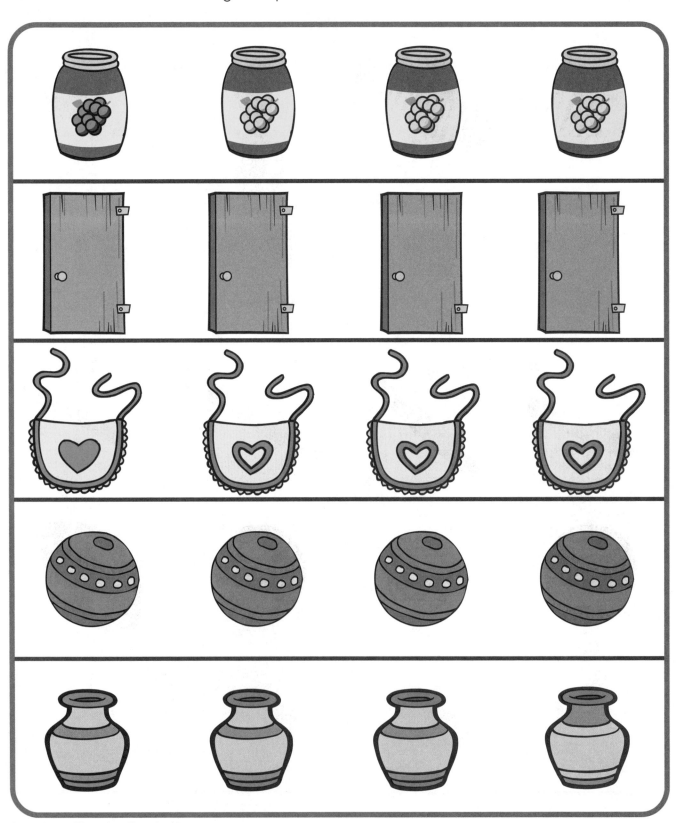

Letter Aa

Directions: Circle the letters that are the same in each row.

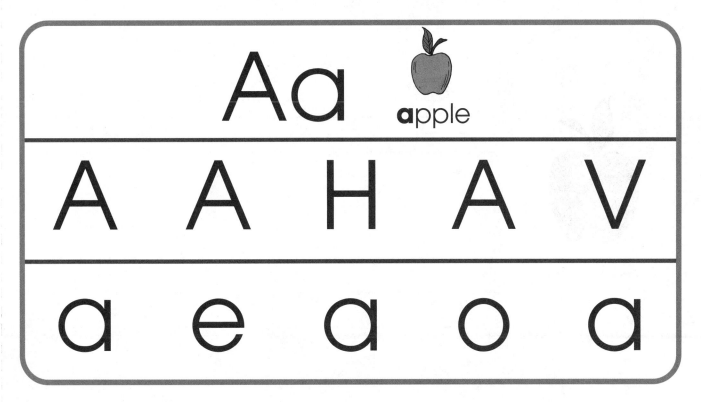

Directions: Circle the letter **a** in each word.

ant   apple   hat

The Sound of Short a

Directions: Trace and write the letters **A** and **a**.

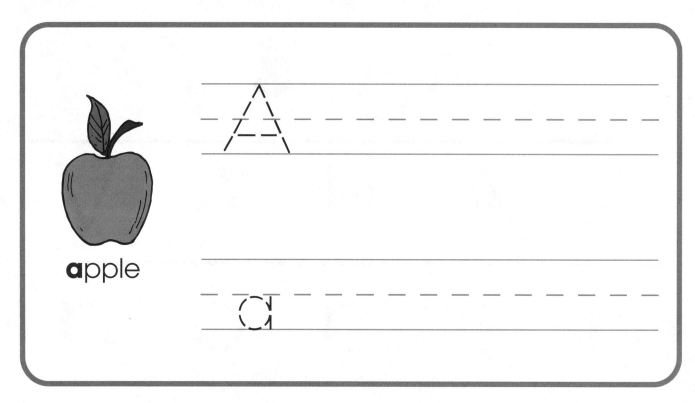

apple

Directions: Say the name of each picture. Circle each picture whose name begins with the same sound you hear at the beginning of **apple**.

The Sound of Short a

hat

Directions: Say the name of each picture. Circle each picture whose name has the same middle sound you hear in the middle of **hat**.

Directions: Circle the picture whose name rhymes with .

Letter Bb

Directions: Circle the letters that are the same in each row.

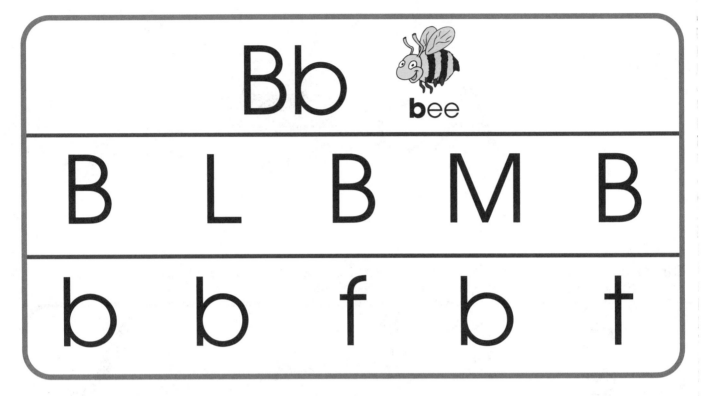

| Bb | bee |

| B | L | B | M | B |

| b | b | f | b | t |

Directions: Circle the letter **b** in each word.

bib   banana   web

The Sound of b

Directions: Trace and write the letters **B** and **b**.

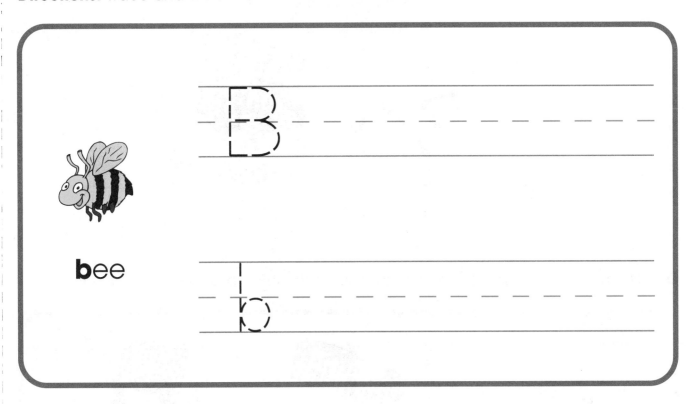

bee

Directions: Say the name of each picture. Circle each picture whose name begins with the same sound you hear at the beginning of **bee**.

The Sound of b

Bb

bee

Directions: Say the name of each picture. Write the letter **b** below each picture whose name begins with the sound of **b**.

Directions: Draw a picture of something whose name begins with the sound of **b**.

Letter Cc

Directions: Circle the letters that are the same in each row.

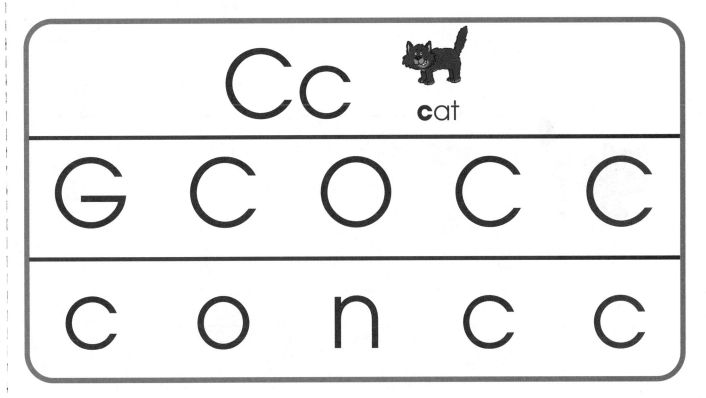

cat

G C O C C

c o n c c

Directions: Circle the letter **c** in each word.

coat   lock   carrot

The Sound of c

Directions: Trace and write the letters **C** and **c**.

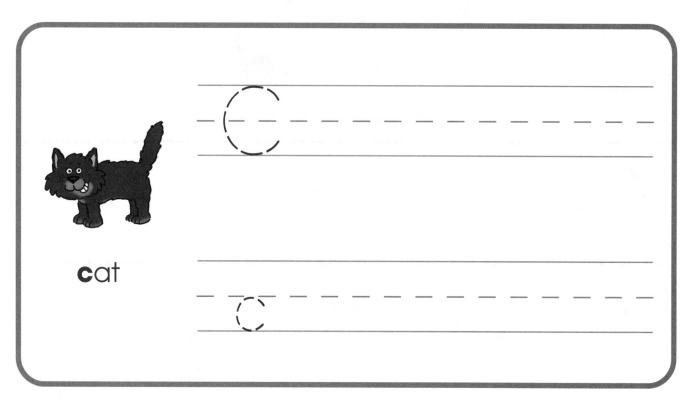

cat

Directions: Say the name of each picture. Circle each picture whose name begins with the same sound you hear at the beginning of **cat**.

The Sound of c

cat

Directions: Say the name of each picture. Write the letter **c** below each picture whose name begins with the sound of **c**.

Directions: Draw a picture of something whose name begins with the sound of **c**.

Letter Dd

Directions: Circle the letters that are the same in each row.

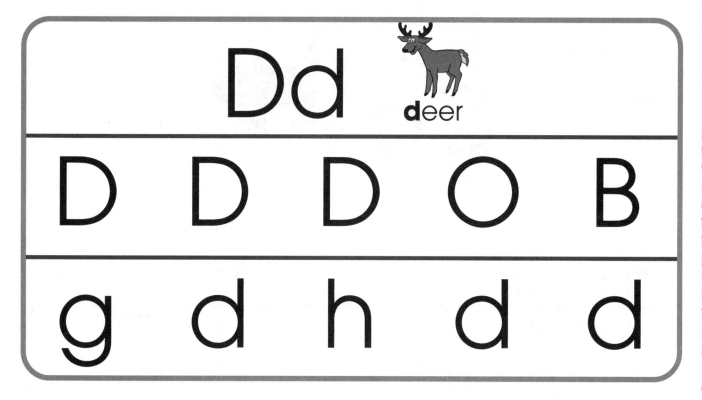

Directions: Circle the letter **d** in each word.

door   desk   bed

The Sound of d

Directions: Trace and write the letters **D** and **d**.

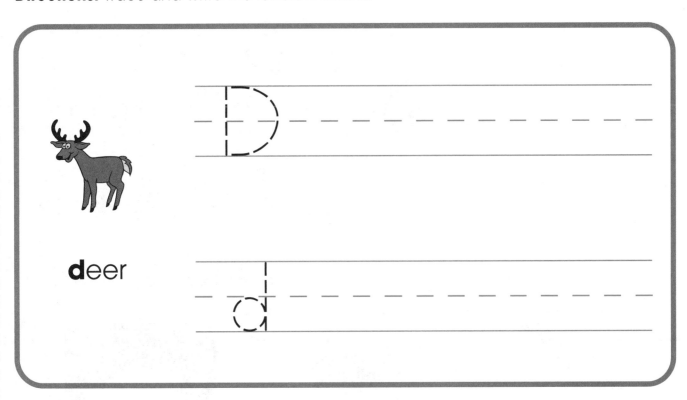

deer

Directions: Say the name of each picture. Circle each picture whose name begins with the same sound you hear at the beginning of **deer**.

The Sound of d

Dd

deer

Directions: Say the name of each picture. Write the letter **d** below each picture whose name begins with the sound of **d**.

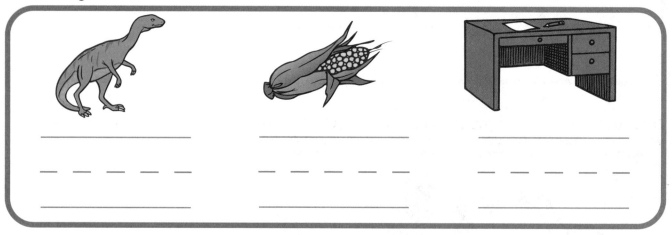

Directions: Draw a picture of something whose name begins with the sound of **d**.

Letter Ee

Directions: Circle the letters that are the same in each row.

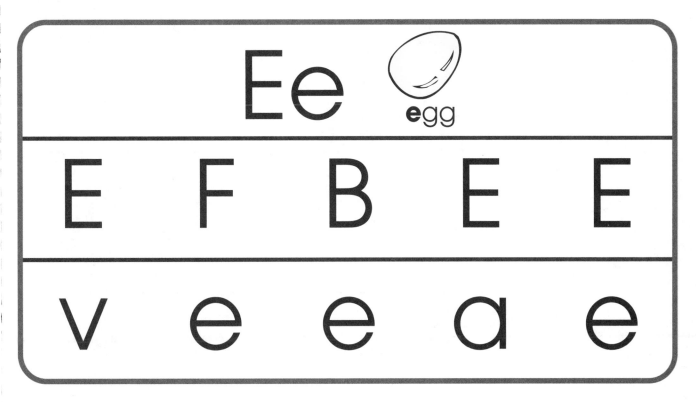

E	F	B	E	E

v	e	e	a	e

Directions: Circle the letter **e** in each word.

elephant   desk   elbow

The Sound of Short e

Directions: Trace and write the letters **E** and **e**.

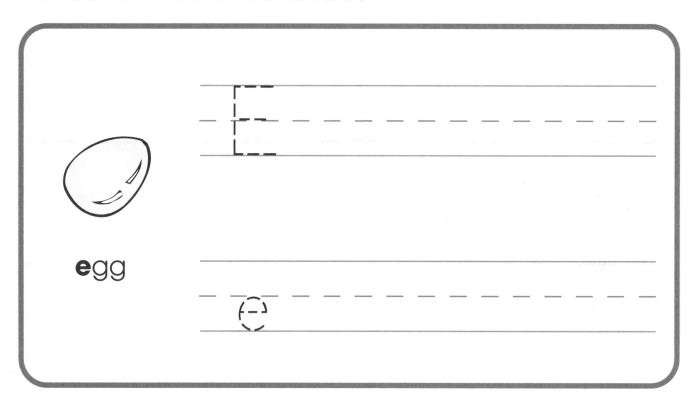

egg

Directions: Say the name of each picture. Circle each picture whose name begins with the same sound you hear at the beginning of **egg**.

The Sound of Short e

Ee **10**
ten

Directions: Say the name of each picture. Circle each picture whose name has the same middle sound you hear in the middle of **ten.**

Directions: Circle the picture whose name rhymes with 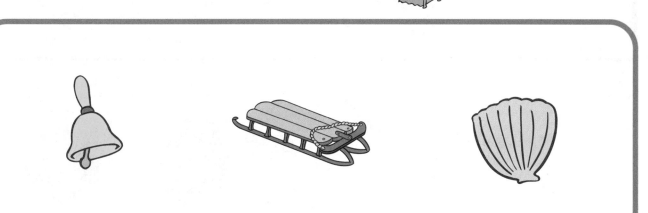.

Vowel Review: Short a and Short e

Directions: Draw an **X** through the picture whose name does **not** begin with the vowel printed at the beginning of each row.

Directions: In each row, draw an **X** through the picture whose name does **not** have the same vowel sound as the names of the other pictures.

Letter Ff

Directions: Circle the letters that are the same in each row.

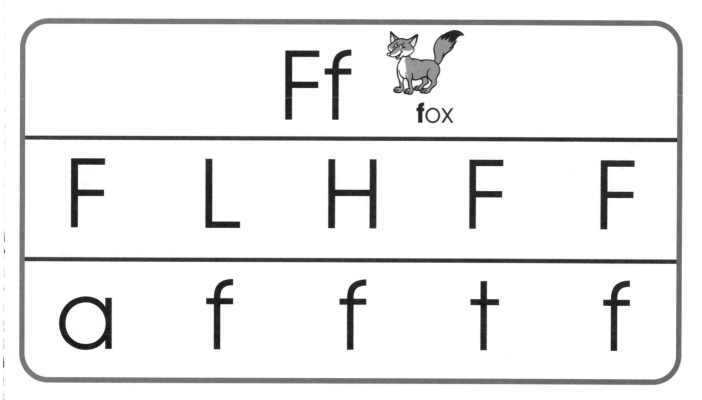

Directions: Circle the letter **f** in each word.

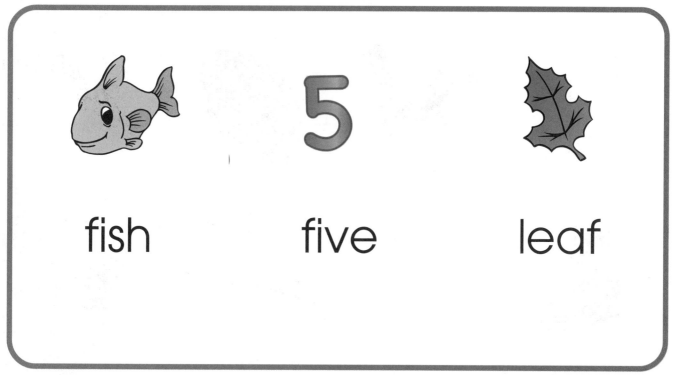

fish   five   leaf

The Sound of f

Directions: Trace and write the letters **F** and **f**.

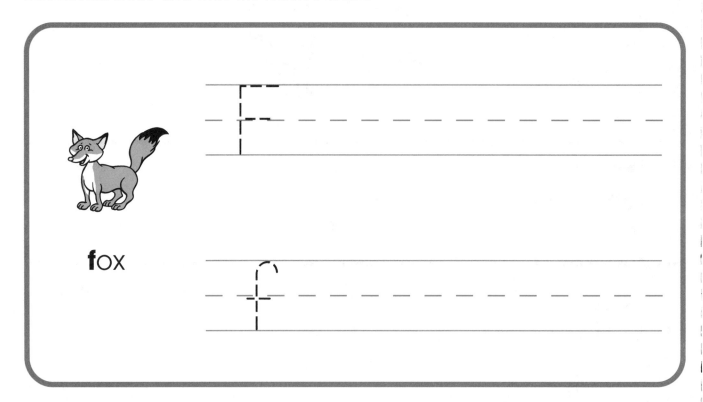

fox

Directions: Say the name of each picture. Circle each picture whose name begins with the same sound you hear at the beginning of **fox**.

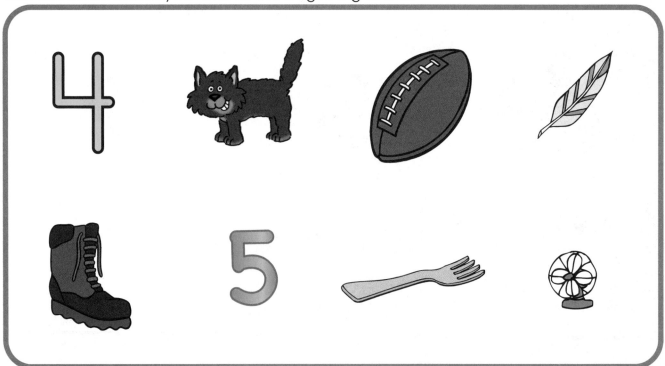

The Sound of f

Ff

fox

Directions: Say the name of each picture. Write the letter **f** below each picture whose name begins with the sound of **f**.

Directions: Draw a picture of something whose name begins with the sound of **f**.

Consonant Review: B, C, D, F

Directions: Draw a line to match each picture name to the letter that shows its beginning sound.

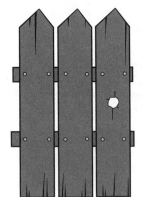

b

c

d

f

Letter Gg

Directions: Circle the letters that are the same in each row.

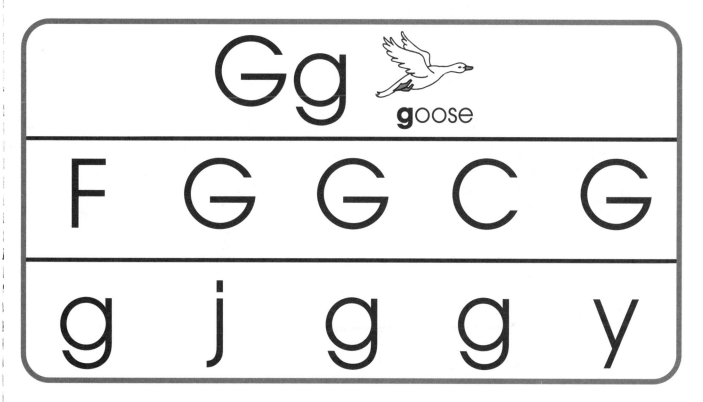

goose

F G G C G

g j g g y

Directions: Circle the letter **g** in each word.

rug   gas   girl

The Sound of g

Directions: Trace and write the letters **G** and **g**.

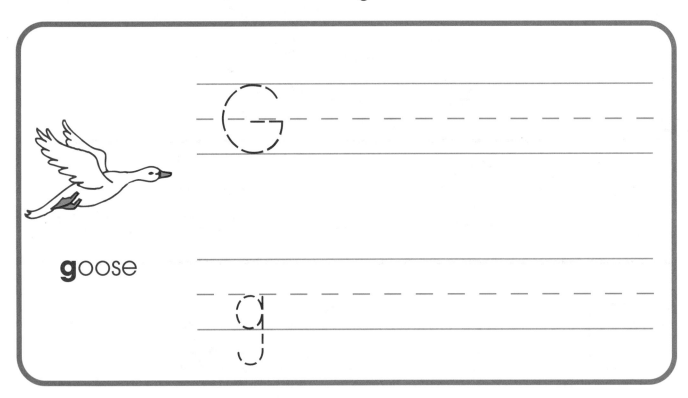

goose

Directions: Say the name of each picture. Circle each picture whose name begins with the same sound you hear at the beginning of **goose**.

The Sound of g

Gg

goose

Directions: Say the name of each picture. Write the letter **g** below each picture whose name begins with the sound of **g**.

------ ------ ------

- - - - - - - - - - - - - - - - - - - - -

------ ------ ------

Directions: Draw a picture of something whose name begins with the sound of **g**.

Letter Hh

Directions: Circle the letters that are the same in each row.

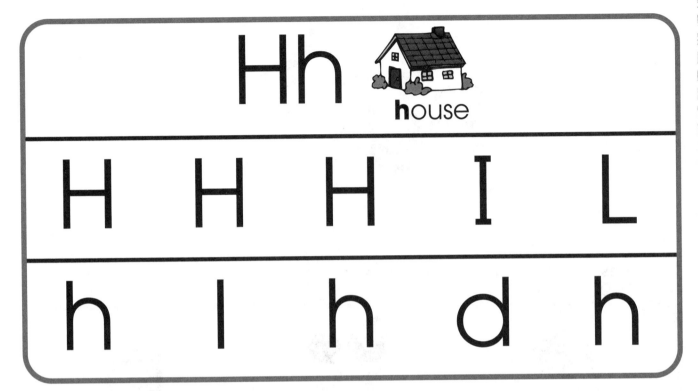

Hh house

H H H I L

h l h d h

Directions: Circle the letter **h** in each word.

hat   ham   brush

The Sound of h

Directions: Trace and write the letters **H** and **h**.

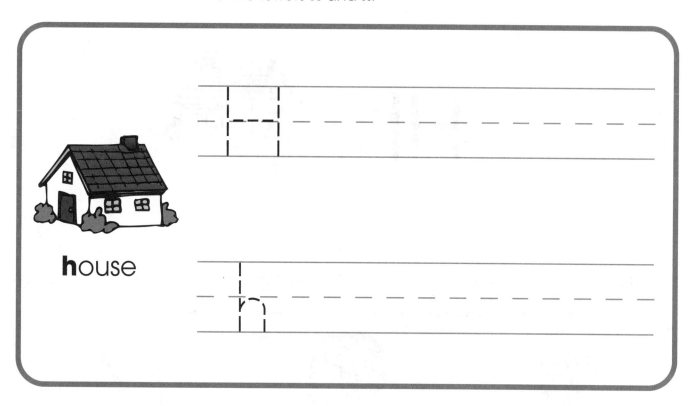

house

Directions: Say the name of each picture. Circle each picture whose name begins with the same sound you hear at the beginning of **house**.

The Sound of h

house

Directions: Say the name of each picture. Write the letter **h** below each picture whose name begins with the sound of **h**.

Directions: Draw a picture of something whose name begins with the sound of **h**.

Letter Ii

Directions: Circle the letters that are the same in each row.

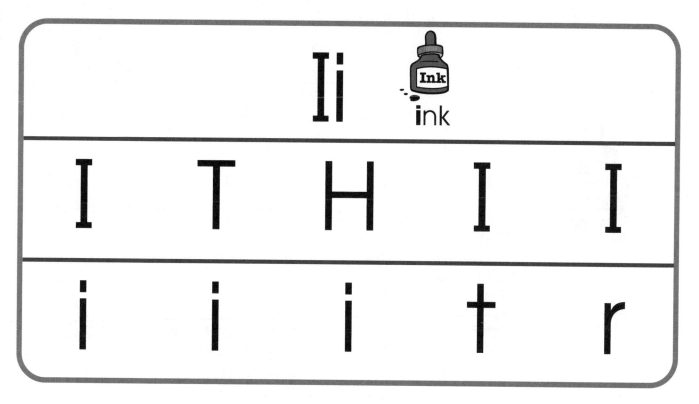

| Ii | ink |

I	T	H	I	I
i	i	i	t	r

Directions: Circle the letter **i** in each word.

igloo   bib   insects

The Sound of Short i

Directions: Trace and write the letters **I** and **i**.

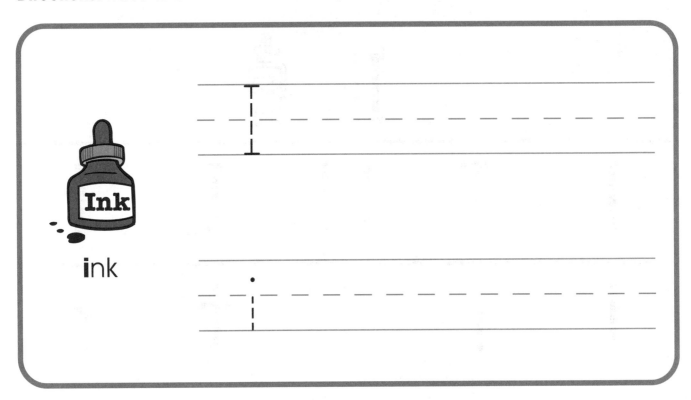

ink

Directions: Say the name of each picture. Circle each picture whose name begins with the same sound you hear at the beginning of **ink**.

Name _____

The Sound of Short i

Ii

pig

Directions: Say the name of each picture. Circle each picture whose name has the same middle sound you hear in the middle of **pig**.

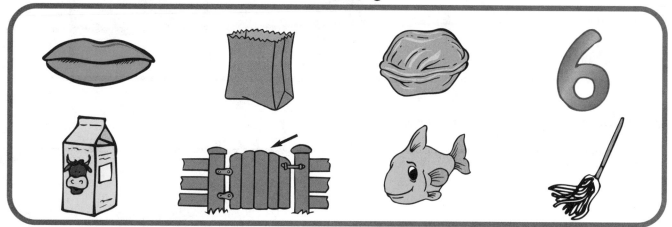

Directions: Circle the picture whose name rhymes with

Letter Jj

Directions: Circle the letters that are the same in each row.

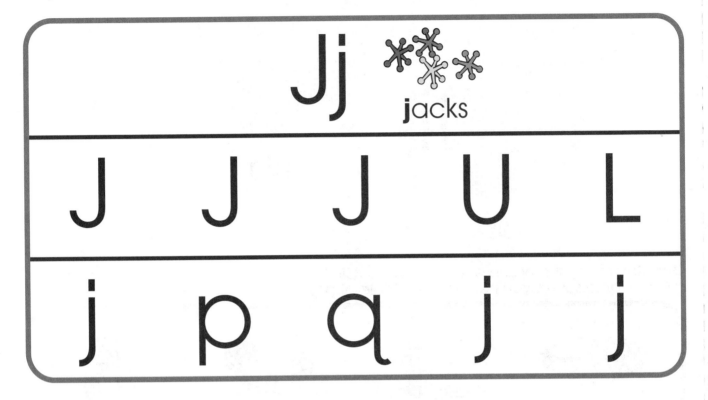

J   J   J   U   L

j   p   q   j   j

Directions: Circle the letter **j** in each word.

jet   jeep   jar

The Sound of j

Directions: Trace and write the letters **J** and **j**.

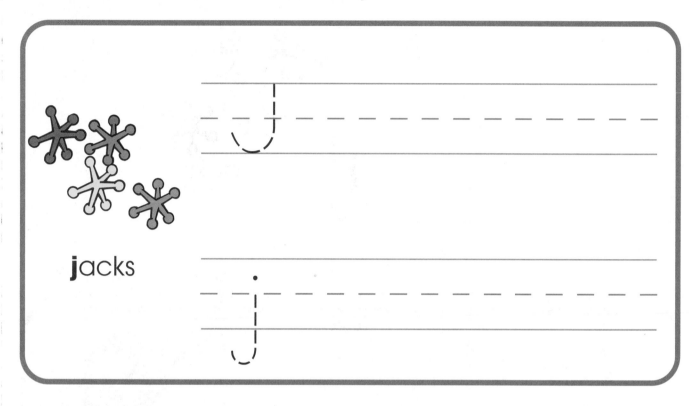

jacks

Directions: Say the name of each picture. Circle each picture whose name begins with the same sound you hear at the beginning of **jacks**.

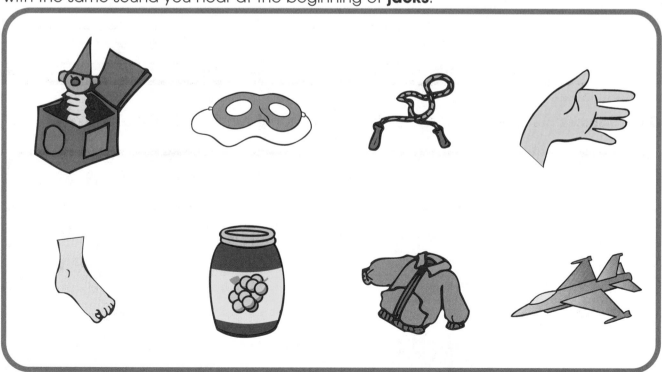

The Sound of j

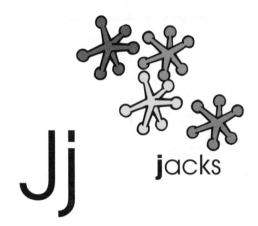

J j jacks

Directions: Say the name of each picture. Write the letter **j**

Directions: Draw a picture of something whose name begins with the sound of **j.**

Letter Kk

Directions: Circle the letters that are the same in each row.

Directions: Circle the letter **k** in each word.

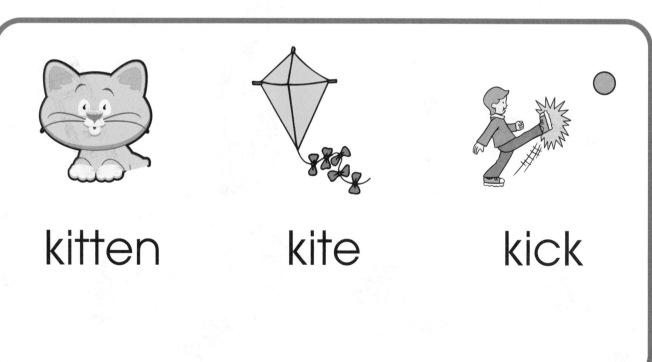

kitten   kite   kick

The Sound of k

Directions: Trace and write the letters **K** and **k**.

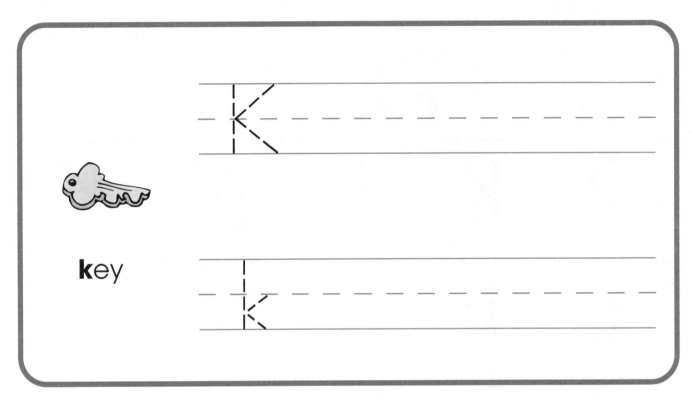

k(ey)

Directions: Say the name of each picture. Circle each picture whose name begins with the same sound you hear at the beginning of **key**.

The Sound of k

Kk 
key

Directions: Say the name of each picture. Write the letter **k** below each picture whose name begins with the sound of **k**.

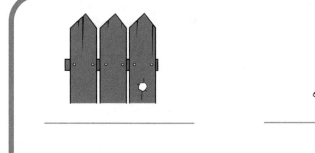

Directions: Draw a picture of something whose name begins with the sound of **k**.

Consonant Review: G, H, J, K

Directions: Draw a line to match each picture name to the letter that shows its beginning sound.

Letter Ll

Directions: Circle the letters that are the same in each row.

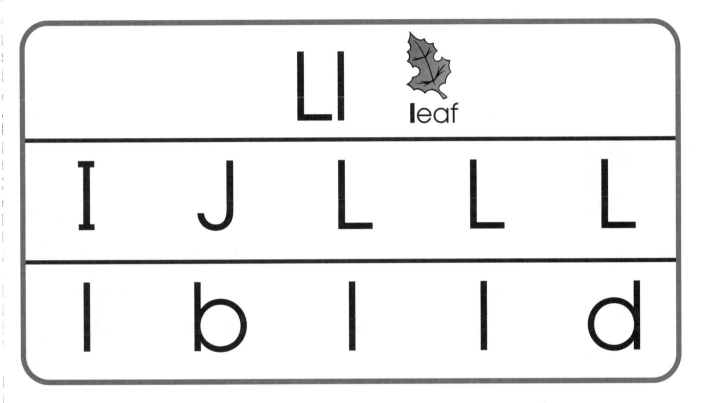

Ll leaf

I J L L L

l b l l d

Directions: Circle the letter **l** in each word.

lion   apple   log

Name

The Sound of l

Directions: Trace and write the letters **L** and **l**.

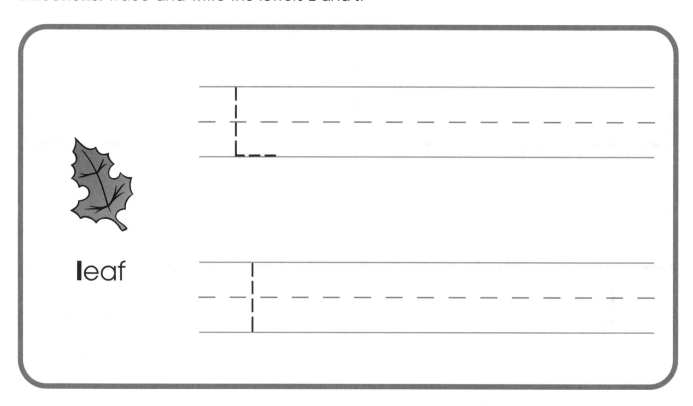

leaf

Directions: Say the name of each picture. Circle each picture whose name begins with the same sound you hear at the beginning of **leaf.**

The Sound of l

leaf

Directions: Say the name of each picture. Write the letter **l** below each picture whose name begins with the sound of **l**.

Directions: Draw a picture of something whose name begins with the sound of **l**.

Letter Mm

Directions: Circle the letters that are the same in each row.

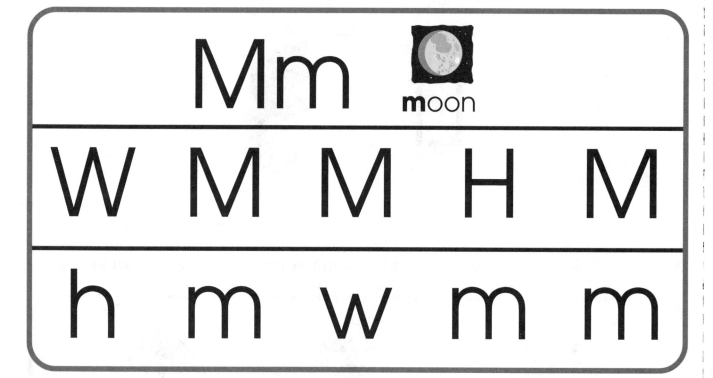

M m

moon

W	M	M	H	M

h	m	w	m	m

Directions: Circle the letter **m** in each word.

mouse   ham   game

The Sound of m

Directions: Trace and write the letters **M** and **m**.

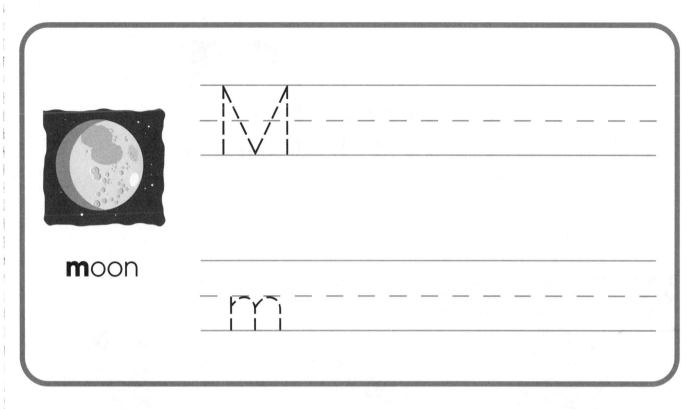

moon

Directions: Say the name of each picture. Circle each picture whose name begins with the same sound you hear at the beginning of **moon**.

The Sound of m

moon

Directions: Say the name of each picture. Write the letter **m** below each picture whose name begins with the sound of **m**.

Directions: Draw a picture of something whose name begins with the sound of **m**.

Letter Nn

Directions: Circle the letters that are the same in each row.

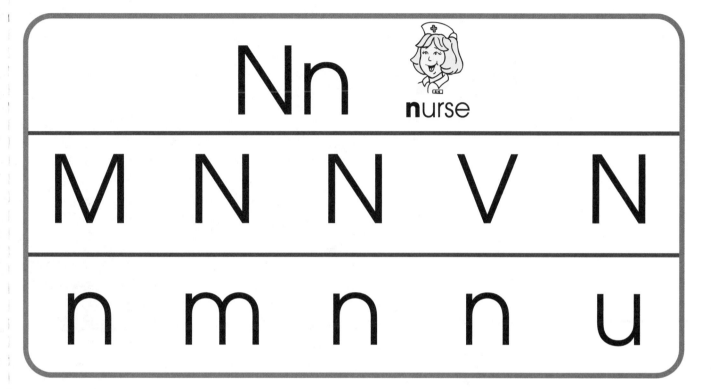

N n	nurse
M N N V N
n m n n u

Directions: Circle the letter **n** in each word.

nest   pen   paint

The Sound of n

Directions: Trace and write the letters **N** and **n**.

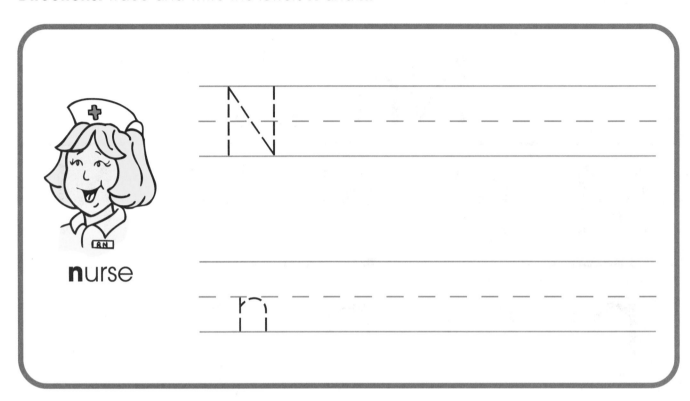

nurse

Directions: Say the name of each picture. Circle each picture whose name begins with the same sound you hear at the beginning of **nurse**.

The Sound of n

Nn

nurse

Directions: Say the name of each picture. Write the letter **n** below each picture whose name begins with the sound of **n**.

Directions: Draw a picture of something whose name begins with the sound of **n**.

Letter Oo

Directions: Circle the letters that are the same in each row.

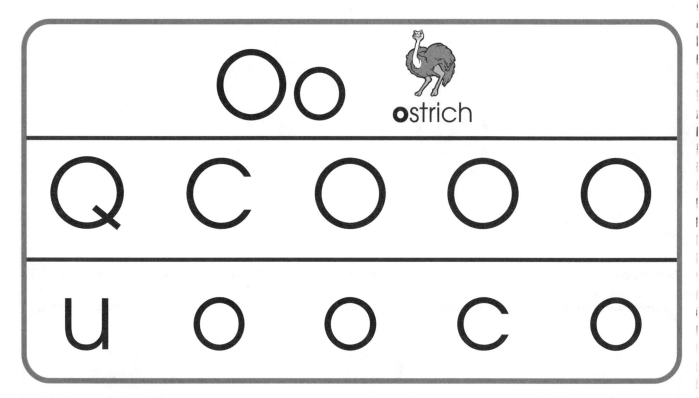

Directions: Circle the letter **o** in each word.

octopus   top   book

The Sound of Short o

Directions: Trace and write the letters **O** and **o**.

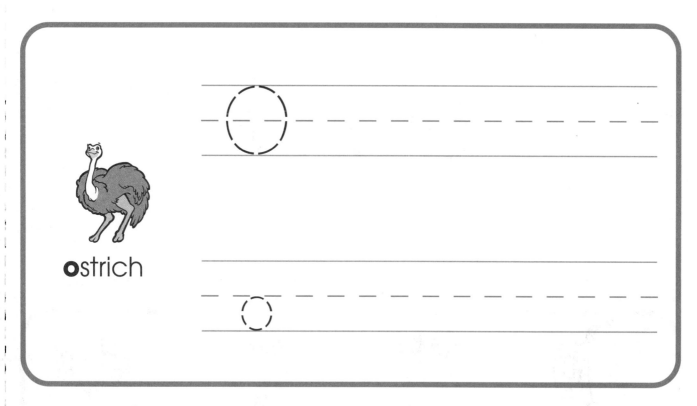

ostrich

Directions: Say the name of each picture. Circle each picture whose name begins with the same sound you hear at the beginning of **ostrich**.

The Sound of Short o

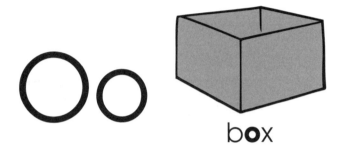

box

Directions: Say the name of each picture. Circle each picture whose name has the same middle sound you hear in the middle of **box.**

Directions: Circle the picture whose name rhymes with .

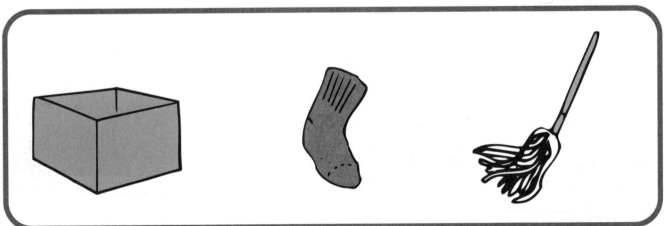

Vowel Review: Short i and Short o

Directions: Draw an **X** through the picture whose name does **not** begin with the vowel printed at the beginning of each row.

Directions: In each row, draw an **X** through the picture whose name does **not** have the same vowel sound as the names of the other pictures.

Letter Pp

Directions: Circle the letters that are the same in each row.

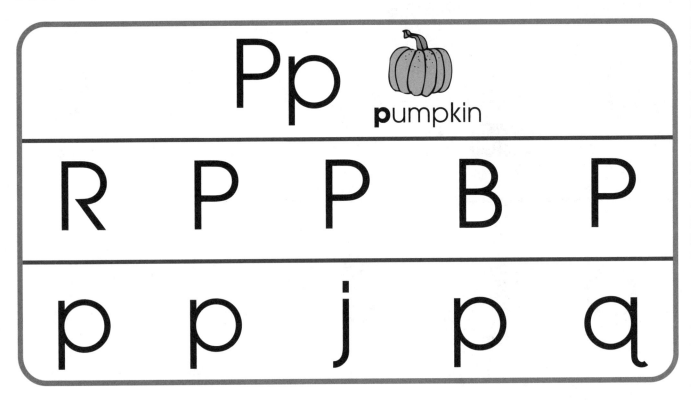

P p **p**umpkin

| R | P | P | B | P |

| p | p | j | p | q |

Directions: Circle the letter **p** in each word.

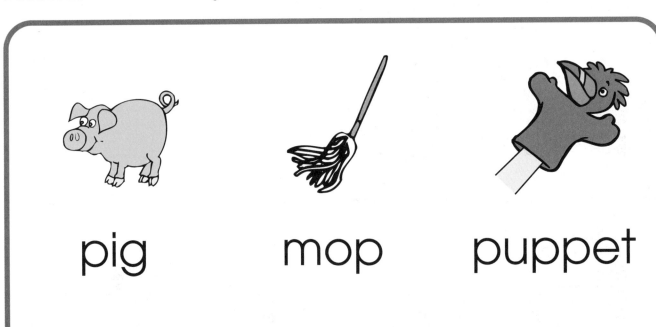

pig   mop   puppet

The Sound of p

Directions: Trace and write the letters **P** and **p**.

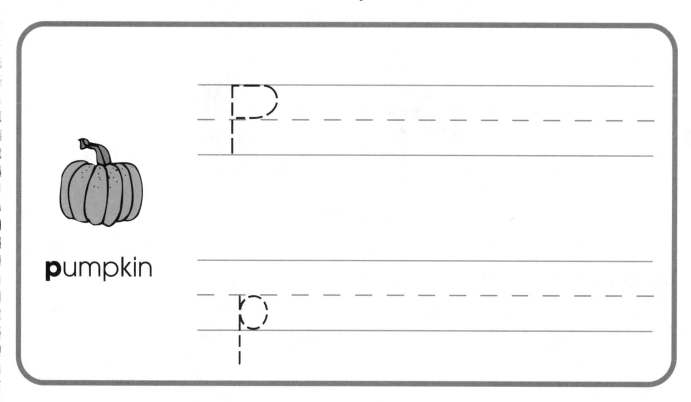

pumpkin

Directions: Say the name of each picture. Circle each picture whose name begins with the same sound you hear at the beginning of **pumpkin**.

The Sound of p

Pp

pumpkin

Directions: Say the name of each picture. Write the letter **p** below each picture whose name begins with the sound of **p**.

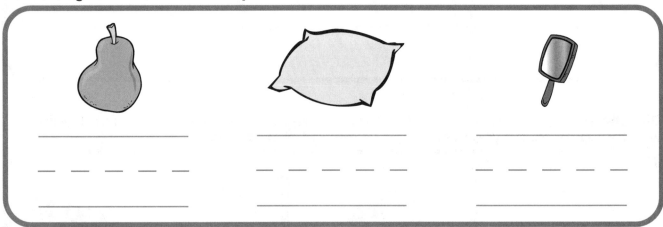

Directions: Draw a picture of something whose name begins with the sound of **p**.

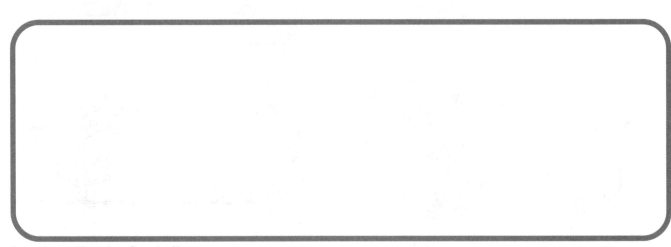

Consonant Review: L, M, N, P

Directions: Draw a line to match each picture name to the letter that shows its beginning sound.

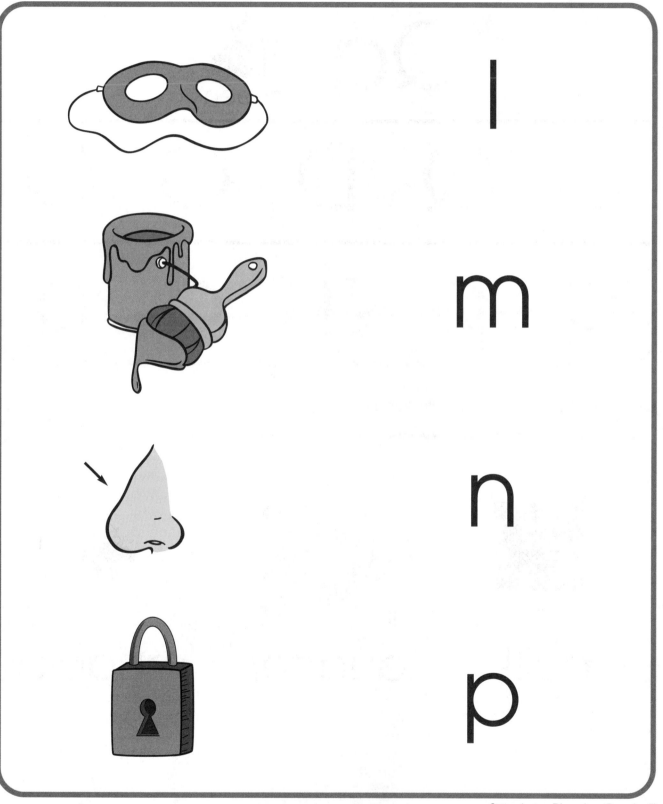

l

m

n

p

Letter Qq

Directions: Circle the letters that are the same in each row.

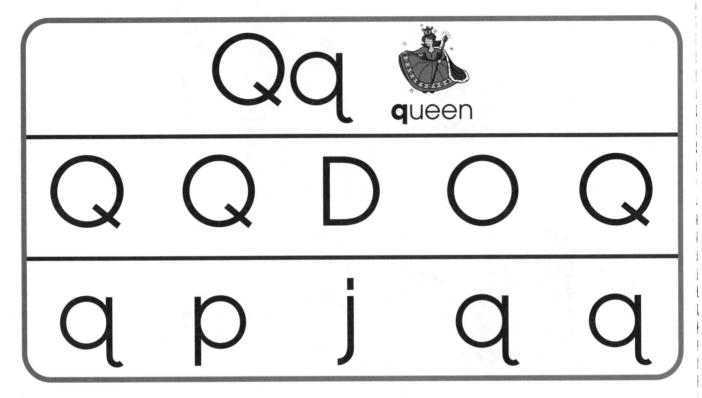

Q Q D O Q

q p j q q

Directions: Circle the letter **q** in each word.

quilt   quarter   quack

The Sound of qu

Directions: Trace and write the letters **Qu** and **qu**.

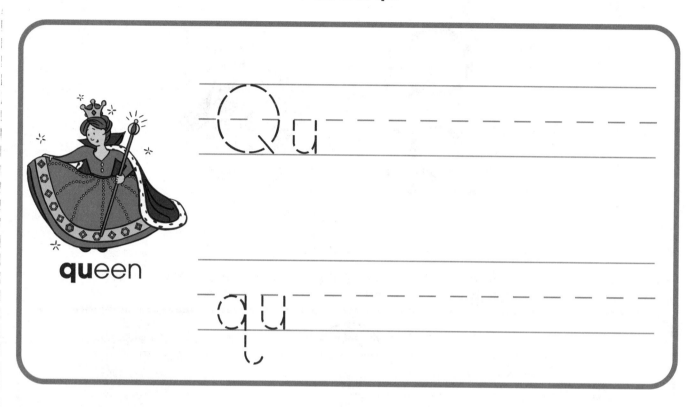

queen

Directions: Say the name of each picture. Circle each picture whose name begins with the same sound you hear at the beginning of **queen**.

The Sound of qu

Qu
qu

queen

Directions: Say the name of each picture. Write the letters **qu** below each picture whose name begins with the sound of **qu**.

Directions: Draw a picture of something whose name begins with the sound of **qu.**

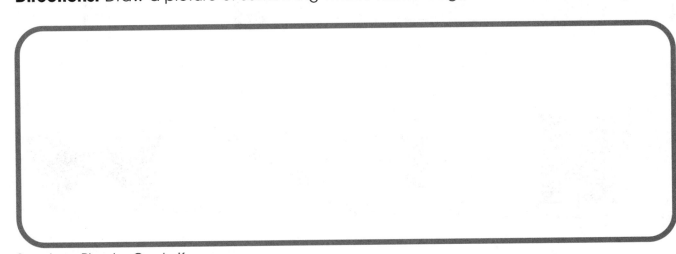

Letter Rr

Directions: Circle the letters that are the same in each row.

Directions: Circle the letter **r** in each word.

rose   bear   yarn

The Sound of r

Directions: Trace and write the letters **R** and **r**.

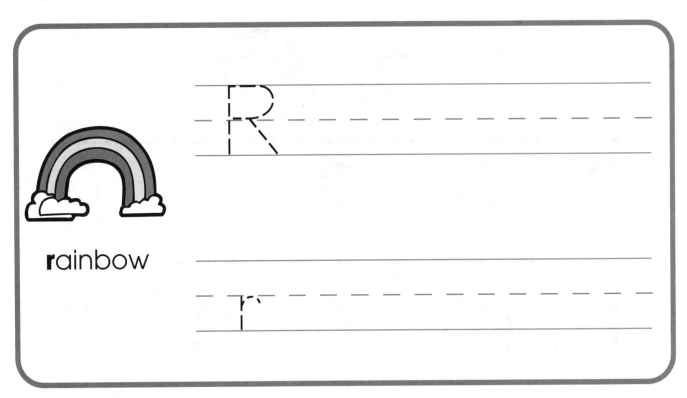

rainbow

Directions: Say the name of each picture. Circle each picture whose name begins with the same sound you hear at the beginning of **rainbow**.

The Sound of r

R r

rainbow

Directions: Say the name of each picture. Write the letter **r** below each picture whose name begins with the sound of **r**.

Directions: Draw a picture of something whose name begins with the sound of **r**.

Letter Ss

Directions: Circle the letters that are the same in each row.

Ss   seal

S	S	G	Z	S
e	s	z	s	s

Directions: Circle the letter **s** in each word.

sun   hose   grass

The Sound of s

Directions: Trace and write the letters **S** and **s**.

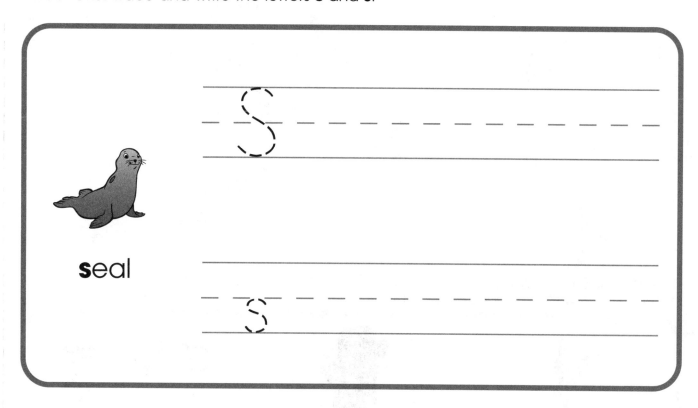

seal

Directions: Say the name of each picture. Circle each picture whose name begins with the same sound you hear at the beginning of **seal**.

The Sound of s

Ss

seal

Directions: Say the name of each picture. Write the letter **s** below each picture whose name begins with the sound of **s**.

Directions: Draw a picture of something whose name begins with the sound of **s**.

Letter Tt

Directions: Circle the letters that are the same in each row.

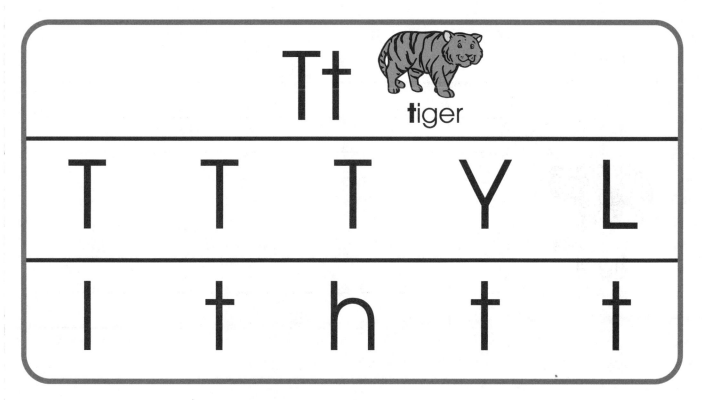

T	T	T	Y	L
I	t	h	t	t

Directions: Circle the letter **t** in each word.

tent   cat   bottle

The Sound of t

Directions: Trace and write the letters **T** and **t**.

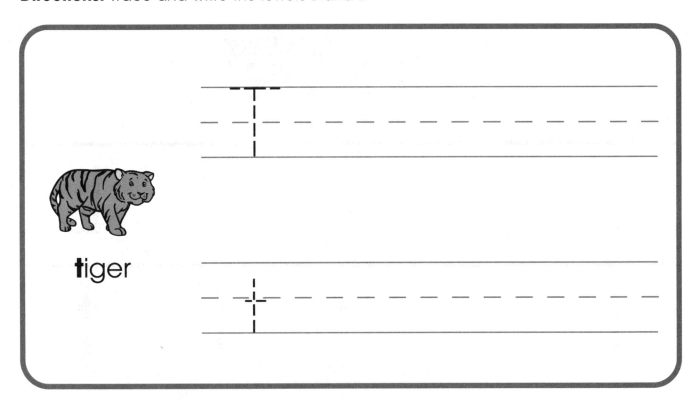

tiger

Directions: Say the name of each picture. Circle each picture whose name begins with the same sound you hear at the beginning of **tiger**.

Name_____

The Sound of t

 Tt

tiger

Directions: Say the name of each picture. Write the letter **t** below each picture whose name begins with the sound of **t**.

_____

_ _ _ _ _ _ _

_____

Directions: Draw a picture of something whose name begins with the sound of **t**.

Consonant Review: Qu, R, S, T

Directions: Draw a line to match each picture name to the letter that shows its beginning sound.

qu

r

s

t

Letter Uu

Directions: Circle the letters that are the same in each row.

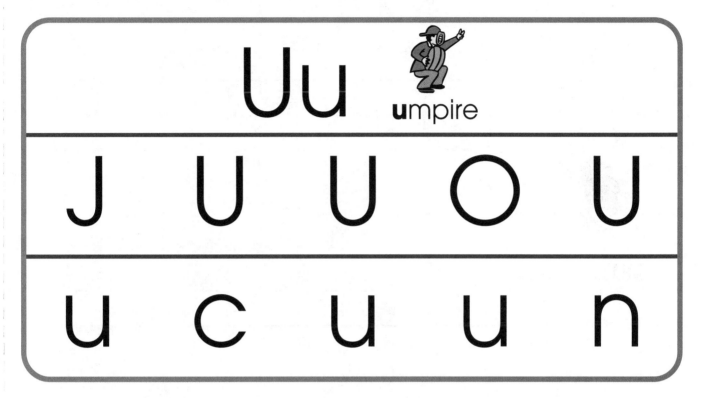

U u   **u**mpire

J U U U O U

u c u u n

Directions: Circle the letter **u** in each word.

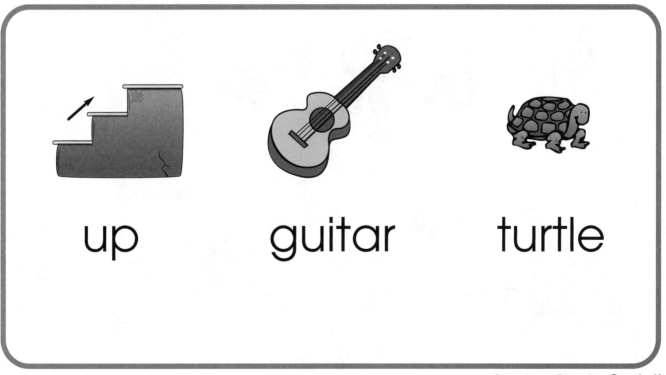

up   guitar   turtle

The Sound of Short u

Directions: Trace and write the letters **U** and **u**.

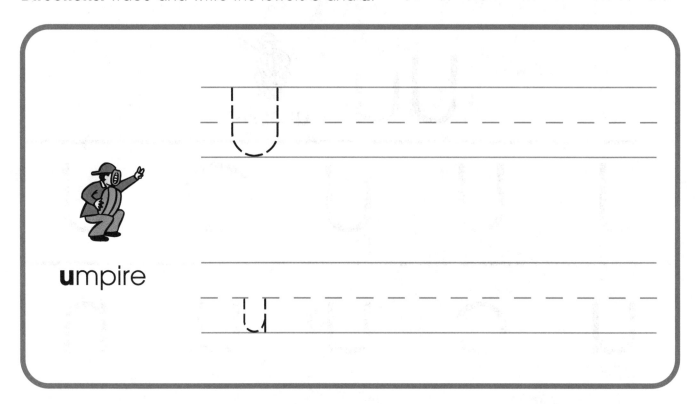

umpire

Directions: Say the name of each picture. Circle each picture whose name begins with the same sound you hear at the beginning of **umpire**.

The Sound of Short u

rug

Directions: Say the name of each picture. Circle each picture whose name has the same middle sound you hear in the middle of **rug**.

Directions: Circle the picture whose name rhymes with

Name _____

Vowel Review: Short u

Directions: Write the letter **u** next to each picture that begins with the short **u** sound.

Directions: Circle each picture whose name has the same middle sound as .

Letter Vv

Directions: Circle the letters that are the same in each row.

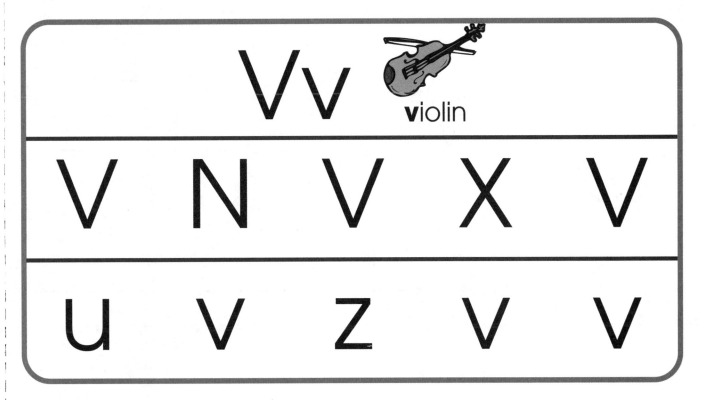

V   N   V   X   V

U   V   Z   V   V

Directions: Circle the letter **v** in each word.

vase   dive   vine

Name_____

The Sound of v

Directions: Trace and write the letters **V** and **v**.

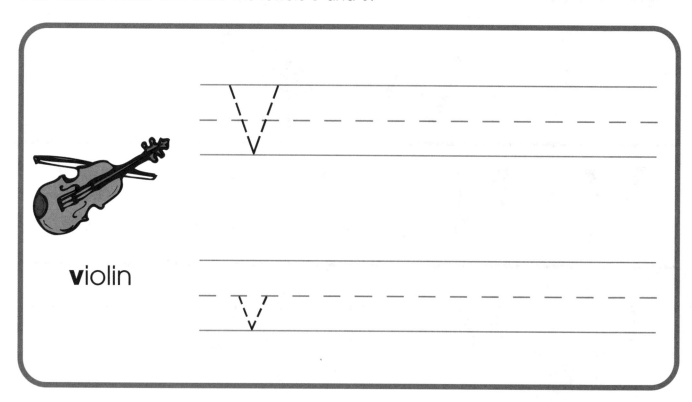

violin

Directions: Say the name of each picture. Circle each picture whose name begins with the same sound you hear at the beginning of **violin**.

The Sound of v

violin

Directions: Say the name of each picture. Write the letter **v** below each picture whose name begins with the sound of **v**.

Directions: Draw a picture of something whose name begins with the sound of **v**.

Letter Ww

Directions: Circle the letters that are the same in each row.

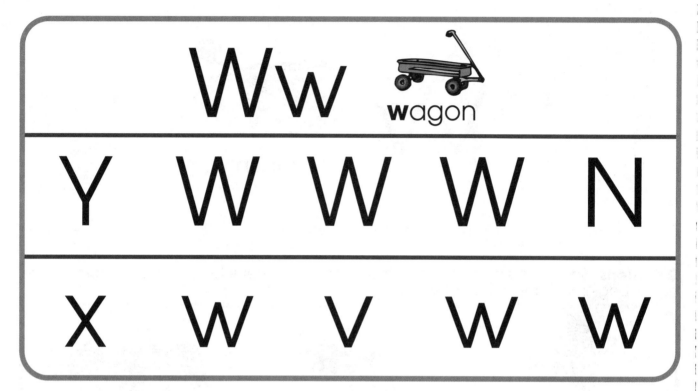

W	w	 **w**agon
Y	W	W	W	N
X	W	V	W	W

Directions: Circle the letter **w** in each word.

watch   window   yawn

The Sound of w

Directions: Trace and write the letters **W** and **w**.

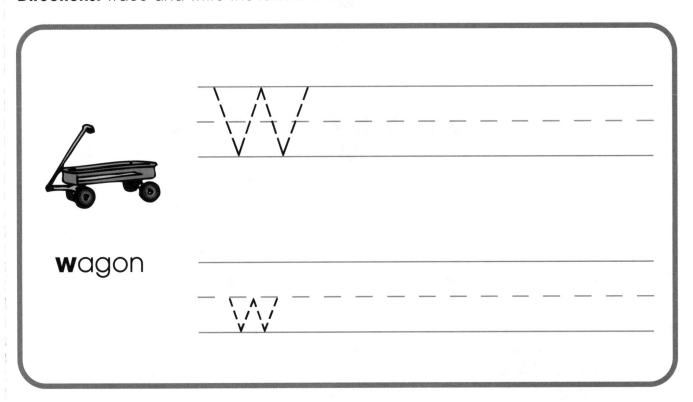

wagon

Directions: Say the name of each picture. Circle each picture whose name begins with the same sound you hear at the beginning of **wagon**.

The Sound of w

wagon

Directions: Say the name of each picture. Write the letter **w** below each picture whose name begins with the sound of **w**.

Directions: Draw a picture of something whose name begins with the sound of **w**.

Letter Xx

Directions: Circle the letters that are the same in each row.

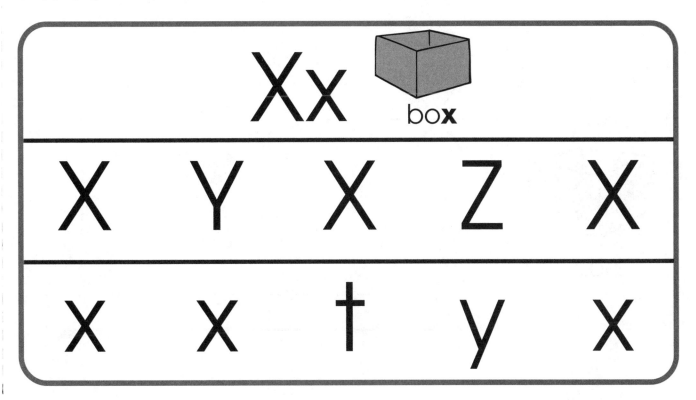

X	Y	X	Z	X
x	x	†	y	x

Directions: Circle the letter **x** in each word.

six   fox   ax

The Sound of x

Directions: Trace and write the letters **X** and **x**.

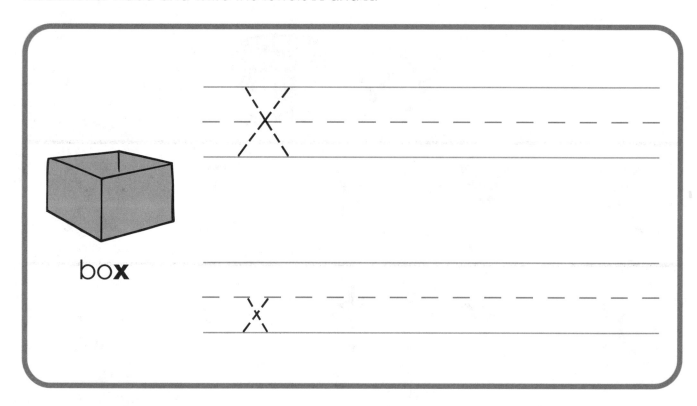

box

Directions: Say the name of each picture. Circle each picture whose name **ends** with the same sound you hear at the end of **box**.

The Sound of x

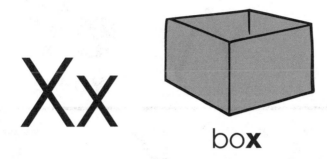

box

Directions: Say the name of each picture. Write the letter **x** below each picture whose name **ends** with the sound of **x**.

Directions: Draw a picture of something whose name **ends** with the sound of **x**.

Letter Yy

Directions: Circle the letters that are the same in each row.

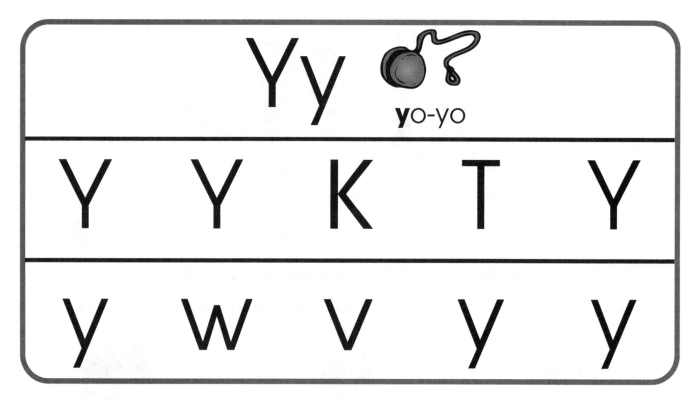

yo-yo

Y	Y	K	T	Y

y	W	V	y	y

Directions: Circle the letter **y** in each word.

yard   yarn   boy

The Sound of y

Directions: Trace and write the letters **Y** and **y**.

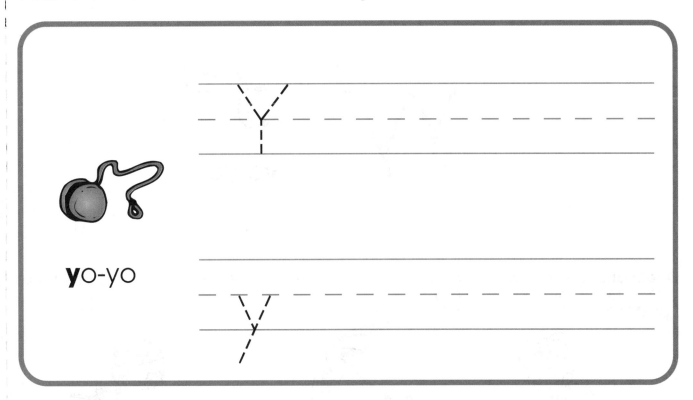

yo-yo

Directions: Say the name of each picture. Circle each picture whose name begins with the same sound you hear at the beginning of **yo-yo**.

Name_____

The Sound of y

Yy

yo-yo

Directions: Say the name of each picture. Write the letter **y** below each picture whose name begins with the sound of **y**.

Directions: Draw a picture of something whose name begins with the sound of **y**.

Spectrum Phonics Grade K

92

Letter Zz

Directions: Circle the letters that are the same in each row.

Zz  **z**ebra

I	Z	N	Z	Z

W	Z	Z	S	Z

Directions: Circle the letter **z** in each word.

zoo   zipper   puzzle

The Sound of z

Directions: Trace and write the letters **Z** and **z**.

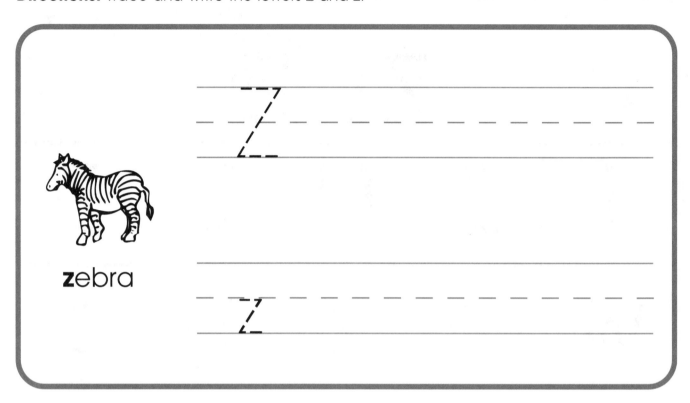

zebra

Directions: Say the name of each picture. Circle each picture whose name begins with the same sound you hear at the beginning of **zebra.**

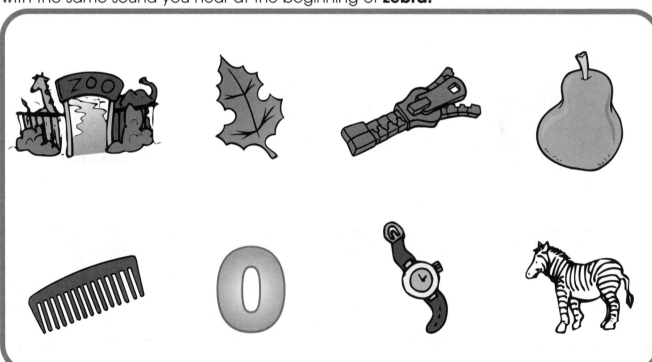

The Sound of z

Zz

zebra

Directions: Say the name of each picture. Write the letter **z** below each picture whose name begins with the sound of **z**.

Directions: Draw a picture of something whose name begins with the sound of **z**.

Consonant Review: V, W, X, Y, Z

Directions: Draw a line to match each picture name to the letter that shows its beginning sound (or ending sound for **x**).

V

W

X

y

Z

Consonant Check-Up

Directions: Write the letter or letters that show the beginning sound of each picture name.

Consonant Check-Up

Directions: Write the letter that shows the beginning sound of each picture name.

Name_____

Vowel Check-Up

Directions: Circle the pictures in each row whose names have the same beginning vowel sound.

Matching Letters

Directions: In each row, circle the letter that is the same as the first letter in the row.

G	O	R	G	B
M	T	P	Y	M
R	N	B	R	I
B	B	O	Y	P
W	A	M	W	B
J	U	C	J	B
T	T	I	L	E

Matching Letters

Directions: In each row, circle the letter that is the same as the first letter in the row.

a	m	a	h	c
d	t	o	d	r
k	w	d	t	k
f	h	t	p	f
q	q	o	g	m
c	o	z	c	g
s	w	s	m	a

Recognizing Letters

Directions: In each row, circle the letters that go with the first letter in the row.

S	p	s	t	s
f	T	O	F	F
j	J	G	O	J
O	b	o	o	m
P	p	s	t	p
I	z	i	t	i
m	A	M	N	M

Recognizing Letters

Directions: In each row, circle the letters that go with the first letter in the row.

c	C	L	C	O
K	k	p	h	k
t	N	T	T	Z
Y	y	y	z	f
U	u	o	u	n
W	t	w	u	w
v	V	A	B	V

Name _____

Beginning Sounds

Directions: Say the name of each picture. In each row, circle the pictures whose names begin with the same sound as the first picture in the row.

Beginning Sounds

Directions: Say the name of each picture. In each row, circle the pictures whose names begin with the same sound as the first picture in the row.

Name

Ending Sounds

Directions: Say the name of each picture. In each row, circle the pictures whose names **end** with the same sound as the first picture in the row.

Name _____

Ending Sounds

Directions: Say the name of each picture. In each row, circle the pictures whose names **end** with the same sound as the first picture in the row.

Short Vowels

Directions: Look at the letter and name the pictures in each row. Circle each picture whose name has the same short vowel sound the letter makes.

Review: ABC Order

Directions: Trace the letters and write the missing letters to complete the alphabet.

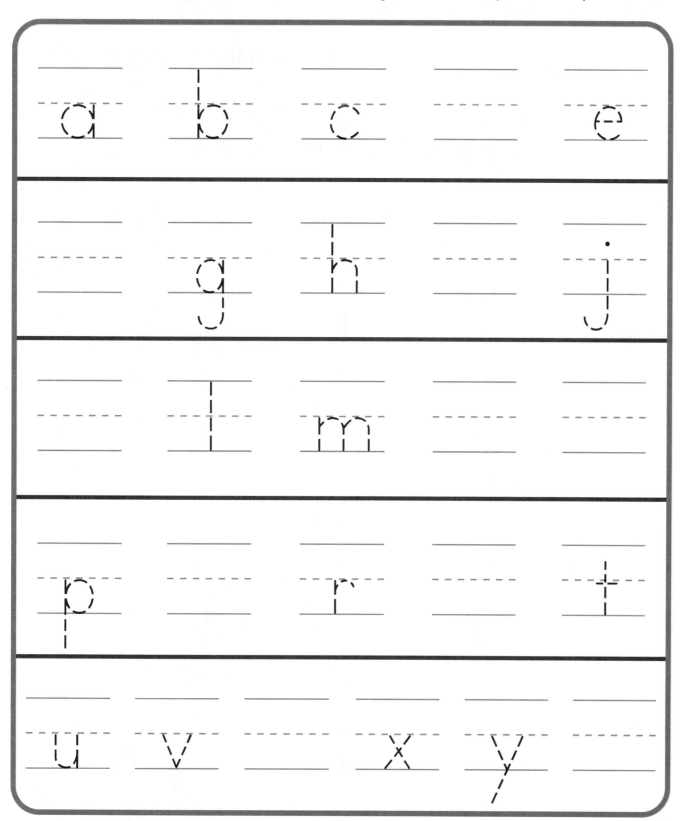

ABC Order

Directions: Trace the letters in each box. Write the missing letters in the blanks. The letters within each box should be in ABC order.

Each letter has its own place in the alphabet.

a b c d e f g h i j k l m
n o p q r s t u v w x y z

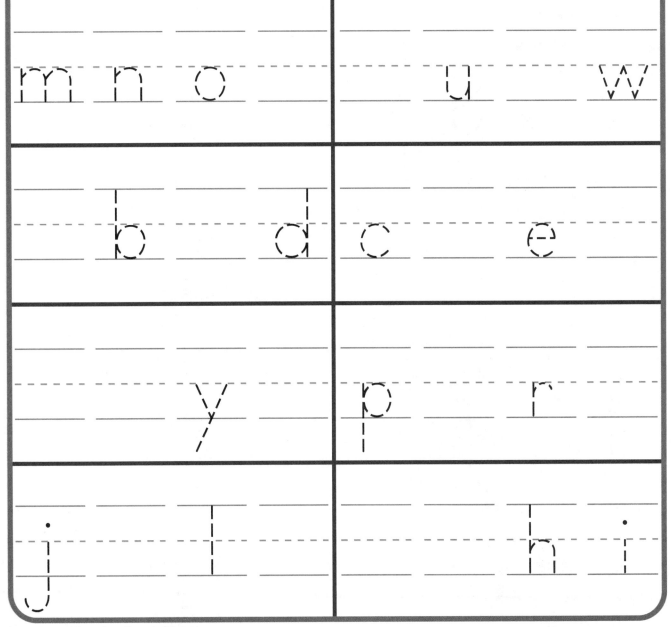

Letters and Their Sounds

apple

bee

cat

deer

egg

fox

goose

house

ink

jacks

key

leaf

moon

Letters and Their Sounds

nurse   **o**strich   **p**umpkin

queen   **r**ainbow   **s**eal

tiger   **u**mpire   **v**iolin

wagon   bo**x**   **y**o-yo   **z**ebra

Practice Page

Practice Page

Answer Key

Name _____

Tracing and Coloring
Directions: Trace the dotted lines to finish the picture. Then, color the picture.

Start here.

6

Name _____

Tracing and Coloring
Directions: Trace the dotted lines to finish the picture. Then, color the picture.

Start here.

7

Name _____

Left to Right
Directions: Trace each dotted line from left to right.

8

Name _____

Same
Directions: Circle the two pictures in each row that are the same.

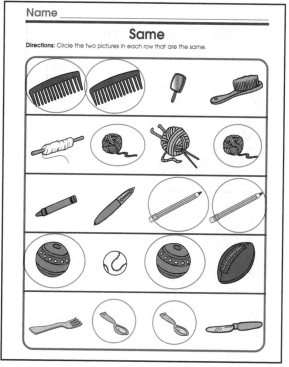

9

Answer Key

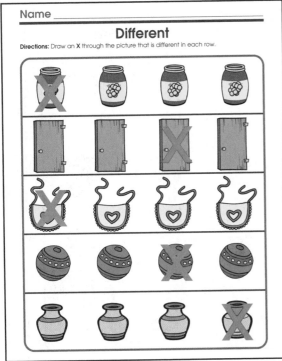

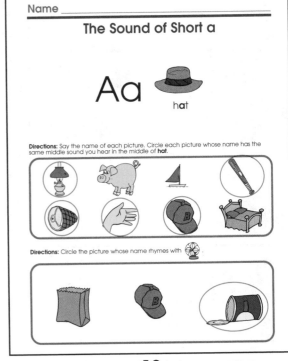

Answer Key

Letter Bb

Directions: Circle the letters that are the same in each row.

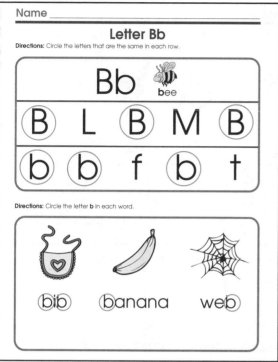

Bb bee

(B) L (B) M (B)

(b) (b) f (b) t

Directions: Circle the letter **b** in each word.

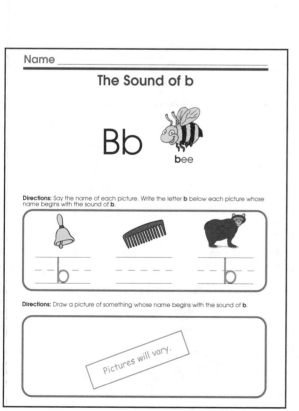

(bib) (banana) (web)

14

The Sound of b

Directions: Trace and write the letters **B** and **b**.

bee

B B B B B

b b b b b b

Directions: Say the name of each picture. Circle each picture whose name begins with the same sound you hear at the beginning of **bee**.

15

The Sound of b

Bb bee

Directions: Say the name of each picture. Write the letter **b** below each picture whose name begins with the sound of **b**.

b ___ ___ b ___

Directions: Draw a picture of something whose name begins with the sound of **b**.

Pictures will vary.

16

Letter Cc

Directions: Circle the letters that are the same in each row.

Cc cat

G (C) O (C) (C)

(c) o n (c) (c)

Directions: Circle the letter **c** in each word.

(c)oat lo(c)k (c)arrot

17

Answer Key

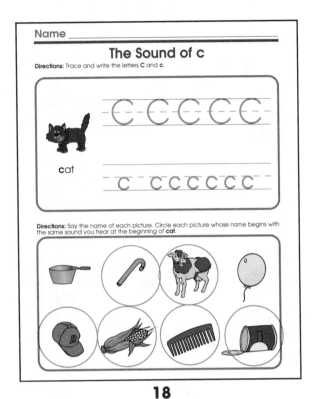

The Sound of c

Directions: Trace and write the letters **C** and **c**.

C C C C C

c C C C C C

cat

Directions: Say the name of each picture. Circle each picture whose name begins with the same sound you hear at the beginning of **cat**.

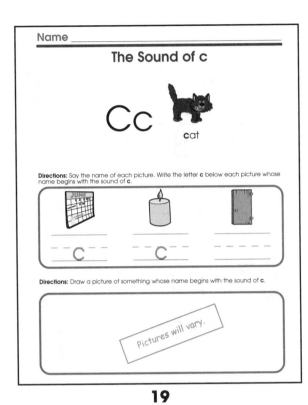

The Sound of c

Cc cat

Directions: Say the name of each picture. Write the letter **c** below each picture whose name begins with the sound of **c**.

c   c

Directions: Draw a picture of something whose name begins with the sound of **c**.

Pictures will vary.

19

Letter Dd

Directions: Circle the letters that are the same in each row.

Dd deer

D D D O B

g d h d d

Directions: Circle the letter **d** in each word.

door   desk   bed

20

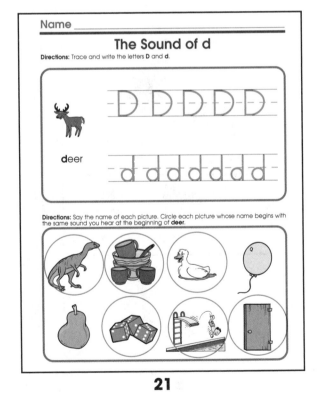

The Sound of d

Directions: Trace and write the letters **D** and **d**.

D D D D D

deer

d d d d d d

Directions: Say the name of each picture. Circle each picture whose name begins with the same sound you hear at the beginning of **deer**.

21

18

Answer Key

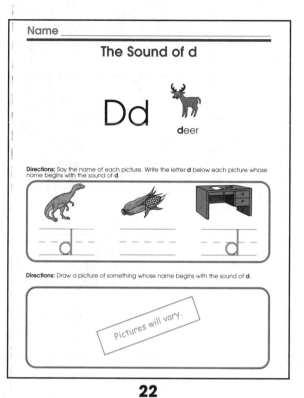

The Sound of d

Dd **d**eer

Directions: Say the name of each picture. Write the letter **d** below each picture whose name begins with the sound of **d**.

d ___ d

Directions: Draw a picture of something whose name begins with the sound of **d**.

Pictures will vary.

22

Letter Ee

Directions: Circle the letters that are the same in each row.

Ee **e**gg

E F B E E

v e e a e

Directions: Circle the letter **e** in each word.

elephant desk elbow

23

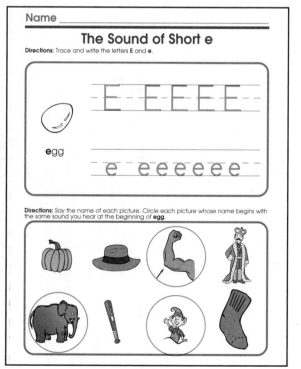

The Sound of Short e

Directions: Trace and write the letters **E** and **e**.

E E E E E

egg

e e e e e e

Directions: Say the name of each picture. Circle each picture whose name begins with the same sound you hear at the beginning of **egg**.

24

The Sound of Short e

Ee 10 ten

Directions: Say the name of each picture. Circle each picture whose name has the same middle sound you hear in the middle of **ten**.

Directions: Circle the picture whose name rhymes with

25

Answer Key

Answer Key

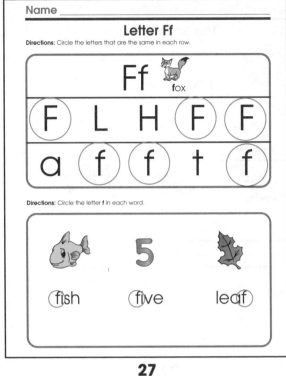

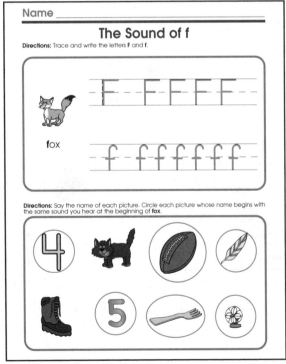

Answer Key

Consonant Review: B, C, D, F

Directions: Draw a line to match each picture name to the letter that shows its beginning sound.

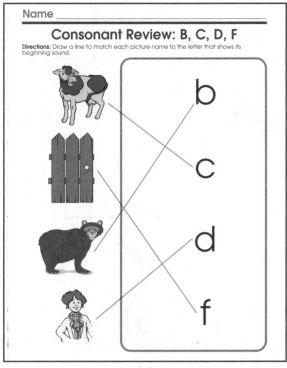

b

c

d

f

30

Letter Gg

Directions: Circle the letters that are the same in each row.

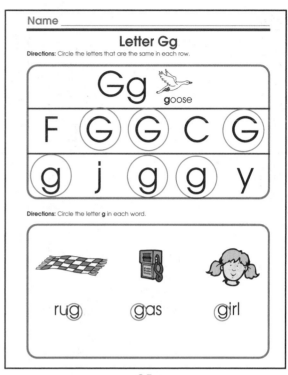

Gg **g**oose

F (G) (G) C (G)

(g) j (g) (g) y

Directions: Circle the letter **g** in each word.

ru(g)   (g)as   (g)irl

31

The Sound of g

Directions: Trace and write the letters **G** and **g**.

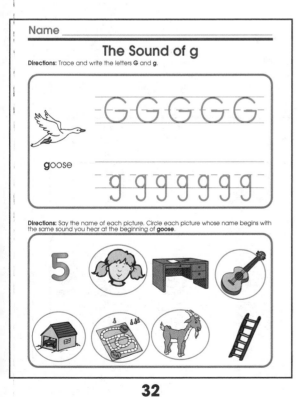

goose

G G G G G

g g g g g g g

Directions: Say the name of each picture. Circle each picture whose name begins with the same sound you hear at the beginning of **goose**.

32

The Sound of g

Gg **g**oose

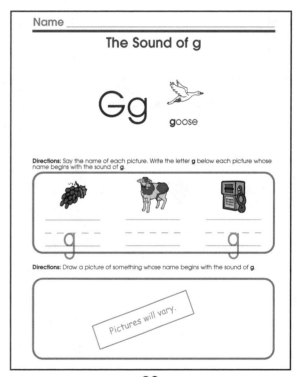

Directions: Say the name of each picture. Write the letter **g** below each picture whose name begins with the sound of **g**.

g _____   _____   _____ g

Directions: Draw a picture of something whose name begins with the sound of **g**.

Pictures will vary.

33

Answer Key

Name _____

Letter Hh

Directions: Circle the letters that are the same in each row.

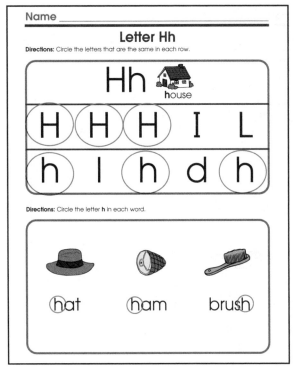

Directions: Circle the letter **h** in each word.

34

Name _____

The Sound of h

Directions: Trace and write the letters **H** and **h**.

Directions: Say the name of each picture. Circle each picture whose name begins with the same sound you hear at the beginning of **house**.

35

Name _____

The Sound of h

Directions: Say the name of each picture. Write the letter **h** below each picture whose name begins with the sound of **h**.

Directions: Draw a picture of something whose name begins with the sound of **h**.

Pictures will vary.

36

Name _____

Letter Ii

Directions: Circle the letters that are the same in each row.

Directions: Circle the letter **i** in each word.

37

Answer Key

Name _____

The Sound of Short i

Directions: Trace and write the letters **I** and **i**.

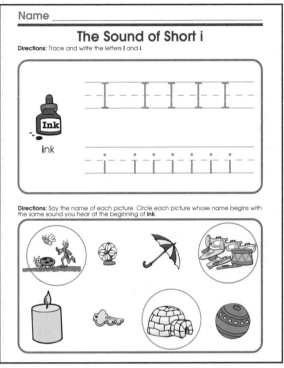

Directions: Say the name of each picture. Circle each picture whose name begins with the same sound you hear at the beginning of **ink**.

38

Name _____

The Sound of Short i

Directions: Say the name of each picture. Circle each picture whose name has the same middle sound you hear in the middle of **pig**.

Directions: Circle the picture whose name rhymes with 🐑

39

Name _____

Letter Jj

Directions: Circle the letters that are the same in each row.

Directions: Circle the letter **j** in each word.

40

Name _____

The Sound of j

Directions: Trace and write the letters **J** and **j**.

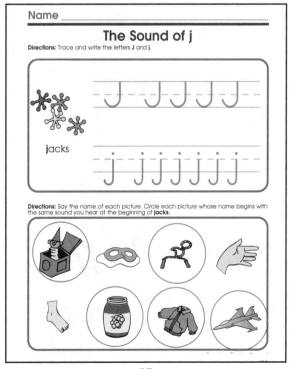

Directions: Say the name of each picture. Circle each picture whose name begins with the same sound you hear at the beginning of **jacks**.

41

Answer Key

Name _____

The Sound of j

Jj

jacks

Directions: Say the name of each picture. Write the letter **j** below each picture whose name begins with the sound of **j**.

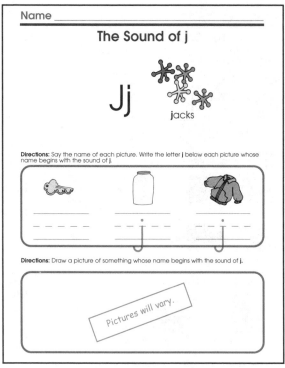

_____ _____ _____
- - j - - - - j - -

Directions: Draw a picture of something whose name begins with the sound of **j**.

Pictures will vary.

42

Name _____

Letter Kk

Directions: Circle the letters that are the same in each row.

Kk key

R (K) (K) N (K)

t (k) l (k) (k)

Directions: Circle the letter **k** in each word.

(k)itten   (k)ite   (k)ick

43

Name _____

The Sound of k

Directions: Trace and write the letters **K** and **k**.

K K K K

key

k k k k k k

Directions: Say the name of each picture. Circle each picture whose name begins with the same sound you hear at the beginning of **key**.

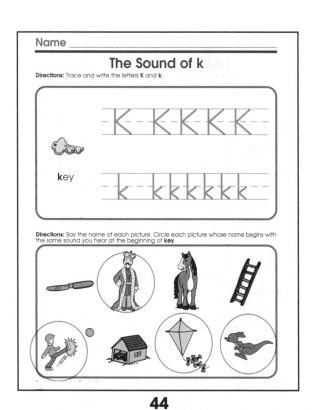

44

Name _____

The Sound of k

Kk key

Directions: Say the name of each picture. Write the letter **k** below each picture whose name begins with the sound of **k**.

_____ _____ _____
        - - k - -   - - k - -

Directions: Draw a picture of something whose name begins with the sound of **k**.

Pictures will vary.

45

Answer Key

Consonant Review: G, H, J, K

Directions: Draw a line to match each picture name to the letter that shows its beginning sound.

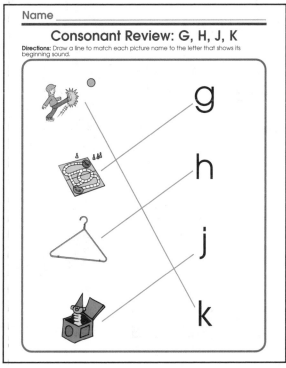

46

Letter Ll

Directions: Circle the letters that are the same in each row.

Ll leaf

| I | J | Ⓛ | Ⓛ | Ⓛ |

| Ⓘ | b | Ⓘ | Ⓘ | d |

Directions: Circle the letter l in each word.

(l)ion   apple   (l)og

47

The Sound of l

Directions: Trace and write the letters L and l.

leaf

Directions: Say the name of each picture. Circle each picture whose name begins with the same sound you hear at the beginning of **leaf**.

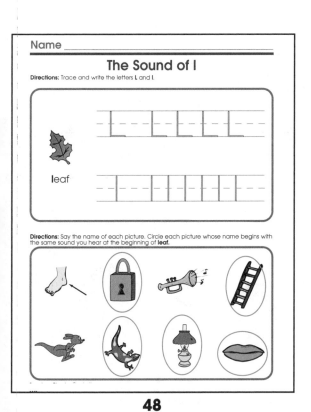

48

The Sound of l

Ll leaf

Directions: Say the name of each picture. Write the letter l below each picture whose name begins with the sound of l.

Directions: Draw a picture of something whose name begins with the sound of l.

Pictures will vary.

49

Answer Key

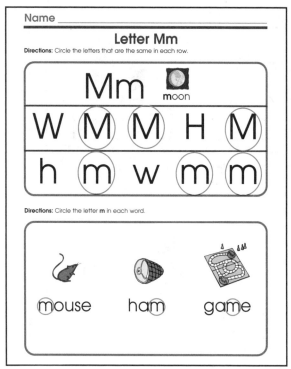

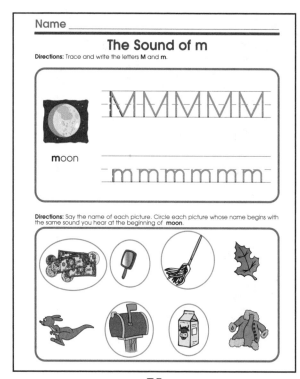

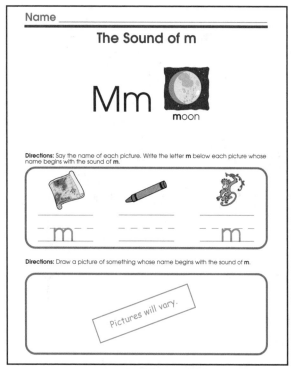

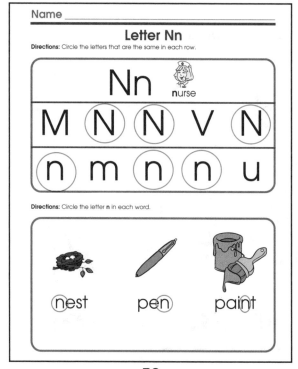

50

51

52

53

Answer Key

Name _____

The Sound of n

Directions: Trace and write the letters **N** and **n**.

nurse

N NNNN

n nnnnnn

Directions: Say the name of each picture. Circle each picture whose name begins with the same sound you hear at the beginning of **nurse**.

54

Name _____

The Sound of n

Nn

nurse

Directions: Say the name of each picture. Write the letter **n** below each picture whose name begins with the sound of **n**.

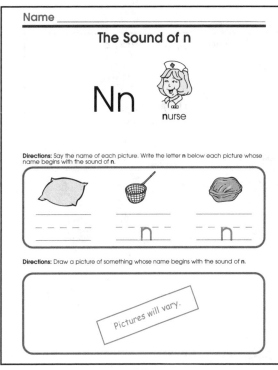

_____ ___n___ ___n___

Directions: Draw a picture of something whose name begins with the sound of **n**.

Pictures will vary.

55

Name _____

Letter Oo

Directions: Circle the letters that are the same in each row.

Oo ostrich

Q C ⊙ ⊙ ⊙

u ⊙ ⊙ C ⊙

Directions: Circle the letter **o** in each word.

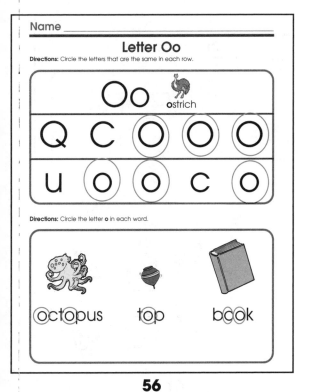

ⓞctopus   tⓞp   bⓞⓞk

56

Name _____

The Sound of Short o

Directions: Trace and write the letters **O** and **o**.

ostrich

O O O O O

o o o o o o

Directions: Say the name of each picture. Circle each picture whose name begins with the same sound you hear at the beginning of **ostrich**.

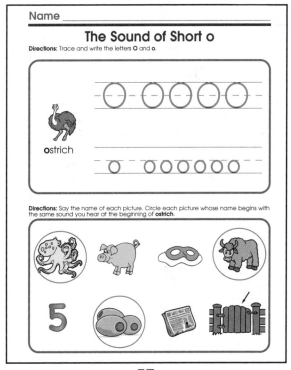

57

Answer Key

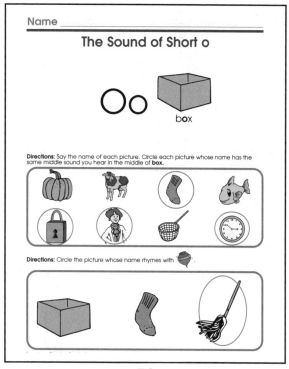

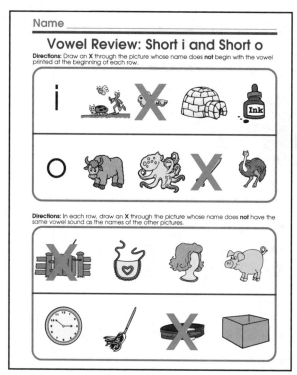

58

59

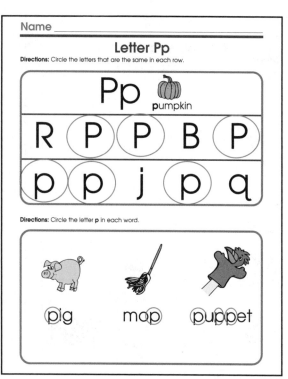

60

61

Answer Key

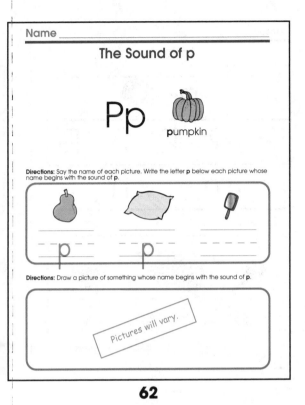

The Sound of p

Pp pumpkin

Directions: Say the name of each picture. Write the letter **p** below each picture whose name begins with the sound of **p**.

p   p

Directions: Draw a picture of something whose name begins with the sound of **p**.

Pictures will vary.

62

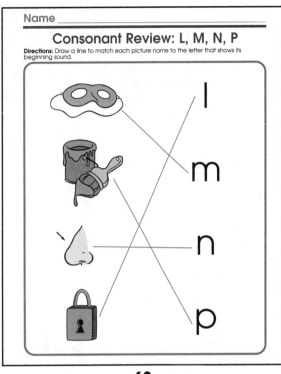

Consonant Review: L, M, N, P

Directions: Draw a line to match each picture name to the letter that shows its beginning sound.

l

m

n

p

63

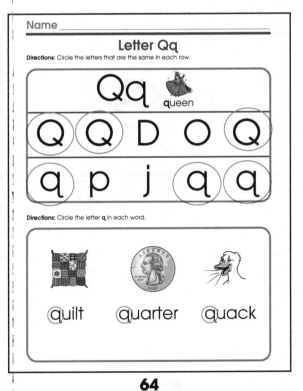

Letter Qq

Directions: Circle the letters that are the same in each row.

Qq queen

Q Q D O Q

q p j q q

Directions: Circle the letter **q** in each word.

quilt   quarter   quack

64

The Sound of qu

Directions: Trace and write the letters **Qu** and **qu**.

queen

Qu Qu Qu

qu qu qu qu

Directions: Say the name of each picture. Circle each picture whose name begins with the same sound you hear at the beginning of **queen**.

65

Answer Key

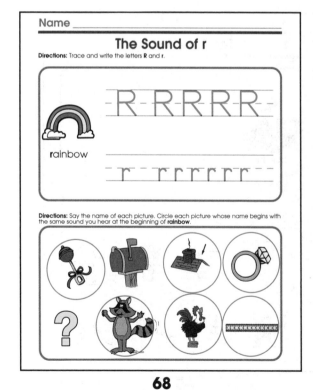

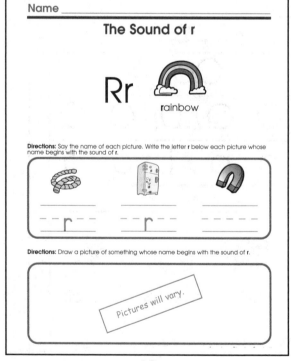

Answer Key

Name _____

Letter Ss

Directions: Circle the letters that are the same in each row.

Directions: Circle the letter **s** in each word.

sun   hose   grass

70

Name _____

The Sound of s

Directions: Trace and write the letters **S** and **s**.

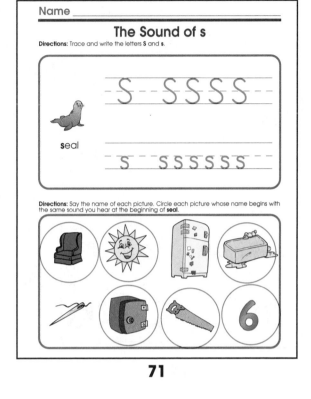

Directions: Say the name of each picture. Circle each picture whose name begins with the same sound you hear at the beginning of **seal**.

71

Name _____

The Sound of s

Ss   seal

Directions: Say the name of each picture. Write the letter **s** below each picture whose name begins with the sound of **s**.

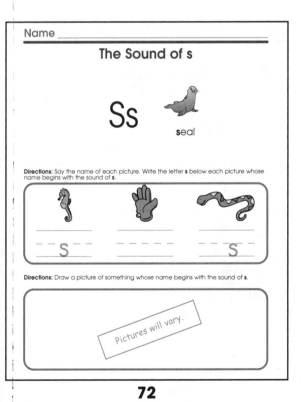

s _____   _____   _____ s

Directions: Draw a picture of something whose name begins with the sound of **s**.

Pictures will vary.

72

Name _____

Letter Tt

Directions: Circle the letters that are the same in each row.

Directions: Circle the letter **t** in each word.

tent   cat   bottle

73

Answer Key

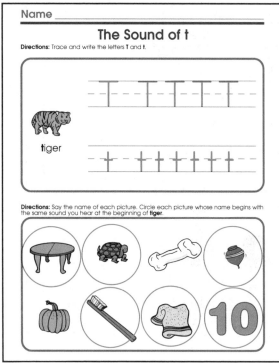

Name _____

The Sound of t

Directions: Trace and write the letters T and t.

tiger

Directions: Say the name of each picture. Circle each picture whose name begins with the same sound you hear at the beginning of **tiger**.

74

Name _____

The Sound of t

Tt   tiger

Directions: Say the name of each picture. Write the letter t below each picture whose name begins with the sound of t.

Directions: Draw a picture of something whose name begins with the sound of t.

Pictures will vary.

75

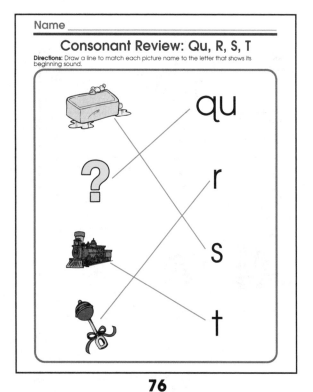

Name _____

Consonant Review: Qu, R, S, T

Directions: Draw a line to match each picture name to the letter that shows its beginning sound.

qu

r

s

t

76

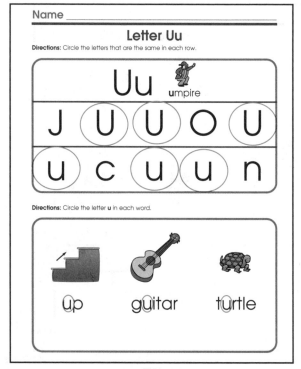

Name _____

Letter Uu

Directions: Circle the letters that are the same in each row.

Uu   umpire

J U U O U

u c u u n

Directions: Circle the letter u in each word.

up   guitar   turtle

77

Answer Key

78

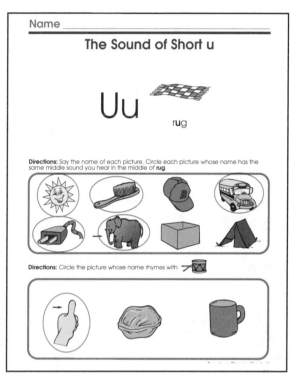

79

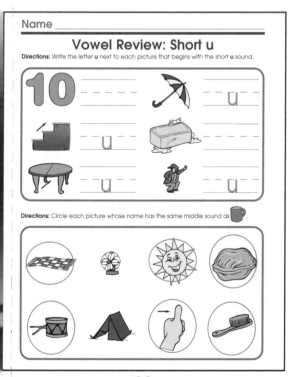

80

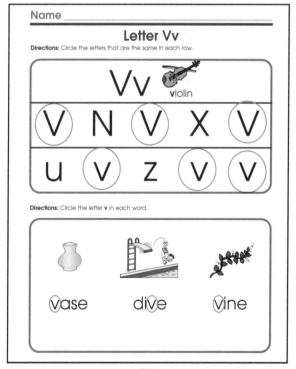

81

Answer Key

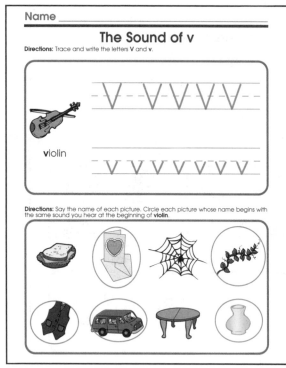

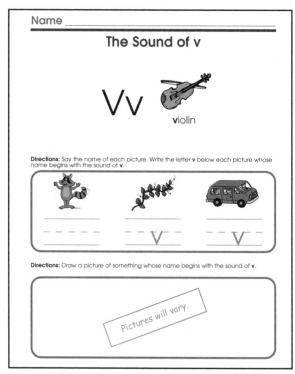

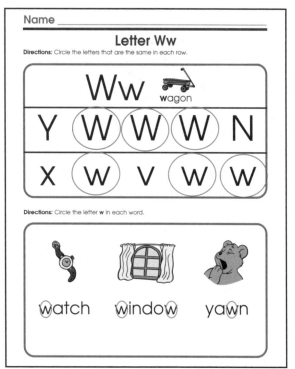

Answer Key

Name _____

The Sound of w

W w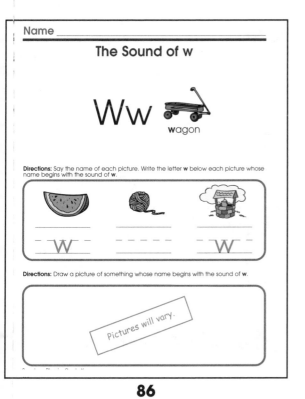
wagon

Directions: Say the name of each picture. Write the letter **w** below each picture whose name begins with the sound of **w**.

___W___   _____   ___W___

Directions: Draw a picture of something whose name begins with the sound of **w**.

Pictures will vary.

86

Name _____

Letter Xx

Directions: Circle the letters that are the same in each row.

Xx box

(X) Y (X) Z (X)

(X) (X) † y (X)

Directions: Circle the letter **x** in each word.

6   fox   ax

si(x)   fo(x)   a(x)

87

Name _____

The Sound of x

Directions: Trace and write the letters **X** and **x**.

box

X X X X X

X X X X X

Directions: Say the name of each picture. Circle each picture whose name **ends** with the same sound you hear at the end of **box**.

88

Name _____

The Sound of x

Xx box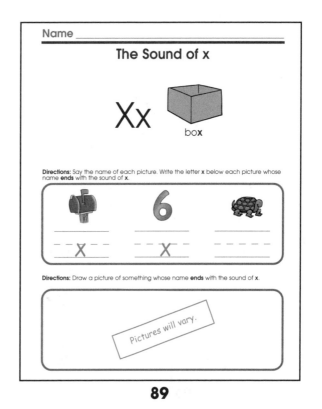

Directions: Say the name of each picture. Write the letter **x** below each picture whose name **ends** with the sound of **x**.

_____   ___X___   ___X___

Directions: Draw a picture of something whose name **ends** with the sound of **x**.

Pictures will vary.

89

Answer Key

Name _____

Letter Yy

Directions: Circle the letters that are the same in each row.

Directions: Circle the letter **y** in each word.

Name _____

The Sound of y

Directions: Trace and write the letters Y and y.

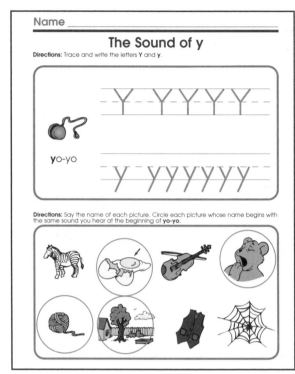

Directions: Say the name of each picture. Circle each picture whose name begins with the same sound you hear at the beginning of **yo-yo**.

90

91

Name _____

The Sound of y

Directions: Say the name of each picture. Write the letter y below each picture whose name begins with the sound of **y**.

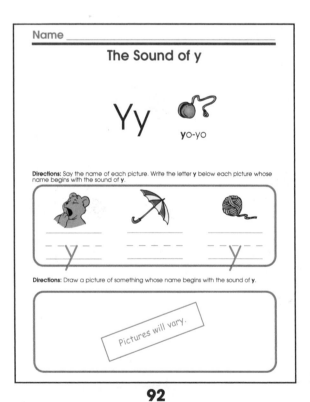

Directions: Draw a picture of something whose name begins with the sound of **y**.

Pictures will vary.

Name _____

Letter Zz

Directions: Circle the letters that are the same in each row.

Directions: Circle the letter **z** in each word.

92

93

Answer Key

Name _____

The Sound of z

Directions: Trace and write the letters **Z** and **z**.

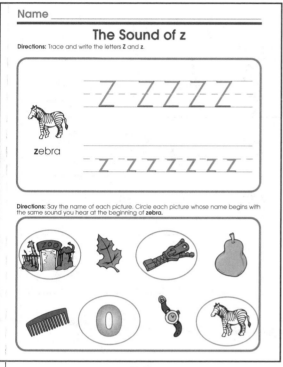

zebra

Z Z Z Z Z Z

Z Z Z Z Z Z Z

Directions: Say the name of each picture. Circle each picture whose name begins with the same sound you hear at the beginning of **zebra.**

94

Name _____

The Sound of z

Zz

zebra

Directions: Say the name of each picture. Write the letter **z** below each picture whose name begins with the sound of **z.**

_____ _____ z

_____ z

Directions: Draw a picture of something whose name begins with the sound of **z.**

Pictures will vary.

95

Name _____

Consonant Review: V, W, X, Y, Z

Directions: Draw a line to match each picture name to the letter that shows its beginning sound (or ending sound for **x**).

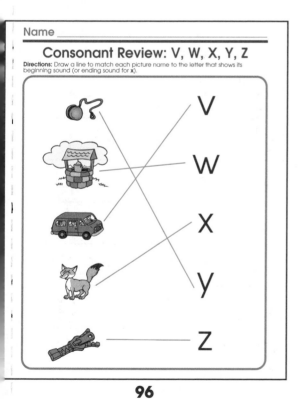

V

W

X

y

Z

96

Name _____

Consonant Check-Up

Directions: Write the letter or letters that show the beginning sound of each picture name.

v

s

t

b

j

k

?

qu

r

z

97

Answer Key

Name _____

Consonant Check-Up

Directions: Write the letter that shows the beginning sound of each picture name.

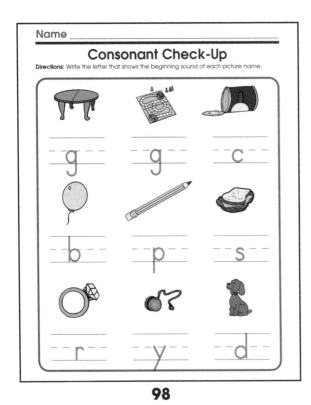

98

Name _____

Vowel Check-Up

Directions: Circle the pictures in each row whose names have the same beginning vowel sound.

99

Name _____

Matching Letters

Directions: In each row, circle the letter that is the same as the first letter in the row.

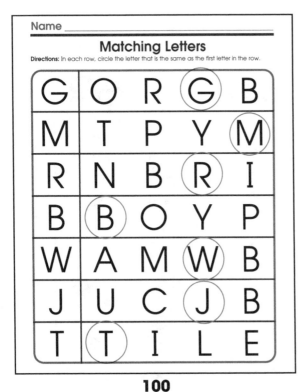

100

Name _____

Matching Letters

Directions: In each row, circle the letter that is the same as the first letter in the row.

a	m	(a)	h	c
d	t	o	(d)	r
k	w	d	t	(k)
f	h	t	p	(f)
q	(q)	o	g	m
c	o	z	(c)	g
s	w	(s)	m	a

101

Spectrum Phonics Grade K

138

Answer Key

Name _____

Recognizing Letters
Directions: In each row, circle the letters that go with the first letter in the row.

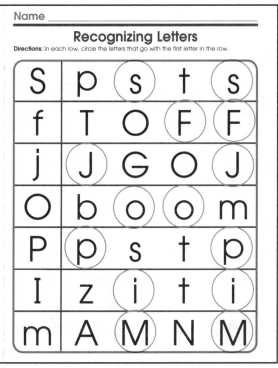

102

Name _____

Recognizing Letters
Directions: In each row, circle the letters that go with the first letter in the row.

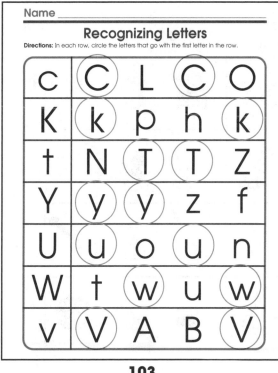

103

Name _____

Beginning Sounds
Directions: Say the name of each picture. In each row, circle the pictures whose names begin with the same sound as the first picture in the row.

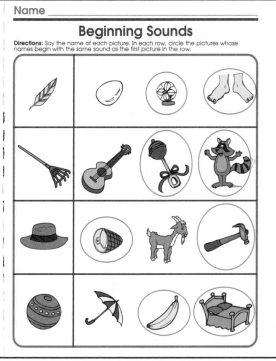

104

Name _____

Beginning Sounds
Directions: Say the name of each picture. In each row, circle the pictures whose names begin with the same sound as the first picture in the row.

105

Answer Key

106

107

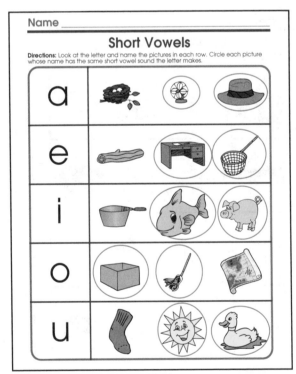

108

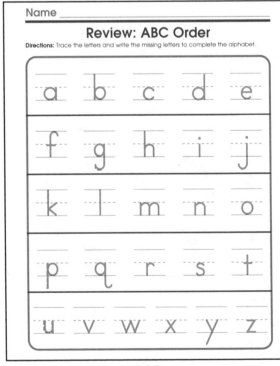

109

Answer Key

Notes

Notes

Notes